ROAD FREAKS

OF

TRANS-AMERIKA

KENNETH LYFTOGT

A ''ProAm'' Book

by

THREE PB PUBLISHING CO. ● 219-221 PARKADE ● CEDAR FALLS, IOWA 50613

Dedicated to

DIANA WINKELMAN

May we grow happier together with age.

ACKNOWLEDGEMENTS

I want to thank...

LOREN TAYLOR for helping me from the start.

MIKE PRAHL and SUE SWEET for help with the manuscript.

PAUL THORNILEY for photography and the twelve pack.

WILLIAM K. SCHROEDER, SANDRA LEE SCHEUER, JEFFREY GLENN MILLER and ALLISON KRAUSE for helping me turn my head around.

GARY BLOBAUM for excellent criticism.

And a whole lot of freaks who gave me floors to sleep on and memories to love.

FOREWORD

"The Radical Era"...some pretty wild times were had by many of us.

You either stayed in your ivory castle and averted your eyes, or you dug your claws into it and fought it to the ground, or... like Ken Lyftogt and thousands of other road freaks... you shot straight through the heart of it, watching the sun set on what America had been and would never be again.

Through it all ran the highway, slicing across the prairies and mountains like so many slashed wrists. It bled on all of us. It fed and poisoned our dreams, shouting adventure, screaming a personal declaration of independence.

It took our children away to strange places and the violent demonstrations that seared and shook the soft, fat underbelly of something the kids called "The Establishment." It was a concrete river that carried and sometimes cast adrift this sub-nation of searchers.

The highway was peopled with a Dickensonian array of characters; the outlaw biker gangs, the gentle commune dwellers, the whores, the hustlers, the saints, the politicos, the rock musicians, the people whose minds were burned away by too many wars, too many drugs, too much highway.

"Where ya' going, son?" "Boy-oh-boy, don't I wish I could travel free like you." "What does that 'Amerika' mean on your pack?" "Why don't you want to settle down?" All echoes from the rest of us, peeking in from the straight world.

And sometimes it was good. Nineteen-year-old good. Sunshine and grass good. Warm, sweet good. Making love good. Bleary-eyed partying good. To a generation of children weaned from sterilized baby bottles and sent out to play in a hygenic, homogenized world, the road seemed like the dying gasp of the romantic cavalier in a workshirt and jeans. You could still battle for an absolute good or square off with hope against an absolute evil.

And sometimes it was lonely as dying. Sometimes the bitterness of wandering jammed in your throat with the hot, midsummer road grime and burned your eyes with tears you'd never cry to irrigate the arid roadbed. Sometimes the cities, the faces, the rides all melted into one, and you'd lie back lost and forgotten, just letting the engine of a stranger's car pull you along. It hurt to be alone, a poet in a chain gang. Cold Montana nights threw memories at your face, stinging you with your own inability or unwillingness to love or be loved. The pack cut welts into your flesh; the pain cut rivulets of sorrow into your mind.

There is much of the highway pounding like a heartbeat through this book, much of the bitter and the sweet. There is much of the concrete and asphalt in Lyftogt's sometimes vitriolic assaults on the rotten, cracking face of so-called ''Amerika,'' in his rapier probe that tries to lance a vicious boil on the backside of a nation.

But look deeper. Walk along the highways of his brutal insight...and if a sun is shining somewhere near the center of you, you might also perceive the gentle flowers in his clenched fist. You may, if you stand quietly at the edge of a garden called ''Trans-Amerika,'' hear that sad, single note of music breaking clear across this land.

Could it be a song of freedom sung by a slave too long oppressed?

Carolyn Barnes

CONTENTS

PART I

BURGIE BURROW

"They glisten in the night,
the memories
of smoke-filled faces
reflected from fire to bottle..."

Lyftogt

ENTRANCE

The waves slapped the shore, one by one, rolling in from far beyond nothing and pulling back into forever. Like the springtime rains washing away the loneliness and cold of winter, the ocean's salty tears waited at the end of the land to clean the soiled wounds of thousands of miles of dust.

The blue-green, white-capped water stretched into long emptiness unmarked by roadsigns and white-striped highways. The shore was an ending for the millions of roads that were Trans-Amerika. Roads running north connected with roads running west, all roads becoming an ending where the waves made their way to the land.

I looked out to the sea, straining to find an impossible end to the gigantic stretch of blue green. Brushing the hair from my eyes, I looked down to my packs laying next to me on the rocky shore. The packs--a bedroll and pack, actually--were both emblazoned with the word "Trans-Amerika."

Idly my fingers traced the letters of the word. Trans-Amerika was a lot of things; a nation of freaks constantly in flux amid the bowels of a larger, more powerful country that spawned an internal ulcer that could someday destroy it. And in the final reel, Trans-Amerika was a declaration of independence for a group of people who were unable to live in a world they never created.

For me, for now, it had become this, a shore, an ending, a time to wash away the pain I felt. She and I had met a few months and a few thousand miles earlier. We had shared the miles, pipes and laughter for a brief time. We'd gone from the warmth of an Iowa campfire to the rage and excitement of the national anti-war demonstrations in Washington, D.C.

But in a small apartment in Oakland, we found that memories of the good times past didn't guarantee the love of times to come.

She had been so beautiful, her long brown hair hung over her shoulders and wandered down her back as she stared silently at the floor. Not a word was spoken as I lashed my packs together across the room from where she sat. We had tried. Not very long and not very hard, but we had at least made an effort. It simply hadn't worked out, and I knew I had better leave and go back to the highways and roadsigns. A closed door became a silent goodbye.

I looked to the sea again, letting the waves wash the memories from my mind. Standing up, I shouldered my packs and turned from the shore to the forest and the mountains. The trees soared above me, as large as I could imagine and as awesome as I could fear. Making my way from one tree to the next, I tried to imagine myself a Daniel Boone or a Tarzan, free human beings, at home in the wilds. I could envision myself living forever among these silent gods of nature, being sheltered and protected by them as I retreated from a hostile world to their strong branches and peaceful shade. Here, beneath the leaves, I could try to forget people, a person, a time and the many miles of road that brought me here.

The forest opened slightly and brought me to Highway 101, the Hippie Highway. North was Carmel and beyond. But here was the forest and the mountains, and I wanted to stay with trees for awhile.

There were other freaks on the road, with packs, beards, knives hanging from leather belts holding up patched jeans. The people of Trans-Amerika, all with lives that the road allowed them to forget. I nodded and smiled as I reached into my pocket for some weed and papers. Finding a soft patch of moss beneath the large trees, I slowly rolled a number, thinking of where I would sleep when it got dark.

I took a deep drag on the number and lay back beneath the tree, holding the smoke deep in my lungs. I looked up at the tree, and marveled at the size of the tree, massive branches that began thirty feet above me and didn't end. The branches and leaves blocked the direct view of the sun; instead, light filtered down to me through the thousands of small, green prisms.

I saw a figure coming toward me. As it approached, I could see it was a man walking with a slight limp and helping himself along with a heavy cane. A combination of beads, sea shells and bells hung from his army-issue knife sheath, and it made soft, tinkling music as he walked. His hair was a bushy blond, hanging down to his shoulders, his face partially hidden by an equally bushy beard. The color of his hair was set off by his eyes, shining blue with a glazed faraway look.

I smiled and handed him the number. He returned the smile and accepted the offer. He took a long hit and held the smoke for a full half minute before he exhaled the smoke.

"You watching for rattlesnakes or scorpions?" he asked, his eyes shining like a man possessed.

"Neither," I answered as I took another deep toke. "People or pigs, not much else."

The stranger laughed and held out his hand, thumb extended, ready to accept the traditional hand clasp of Trans-Amerika. "I'm Doc. Who and what are you? What sign, I mean."

I popped the roach, took his hand and said, "Kenny. I'm a Leo."

"Far out," he answered, shaking his head. "We need a Leo. Come on, that's all we're missing."

So we made our way alond the road. "Kenny, huh?" said Doc. "I take it you just got in?"

"Yeah," I mumbled. "Was by the bay yesterday, you know, Oakland and Berkely."

"I like it there too," he answered. "Good place. I'm from Boston and New Jersey. Used to ride with a club there, Henchmen. Man, we were a wild bunch of mothers." Laughing, he glanced at me. "You ever heard of them?"

"No," I grinned, "I generally stay clear of the biker packs."

He laughed and slapped me on the back. "That's a good way to stay in one piece, especially if you're not tight with any members." His voice drifted off as he continued, "Yeah, we had some far-out times, but I wrecked my chop and then left New Jersey when I got out of the hospital."

"That's why the cane?" I asked.

"This?!" he said stopping for a second and holding it up for inspection. "Hell no, I'm a damn Vietnam veteran. Yeah, believe me, man!" Then, slapping the cane against his injured leg, he continued, "This fucking leg's got about two ounces of Chinese shrapnel still in it! That's what I got for getting drafted into good citizenship. Screw that crap. I'm a veteran against the war. I'll let this country blow up before I'll ever cross an ocean to kill some dude who don't even know me. Christ, I make enough enemies right here at home! Yeah," his voice grew even more serious and calm as we walked along. "Since I got out, I've helped organize a lot of demonstrations against it, but the war's still on, so to hell with it all! That's what I say, to hell with it all! These mountains are good enough for me. No hassles, no nothin'."

"Yeah," I said, looking at the ground, "maybe you're right, to hell with it."

"Time out!" He laughed and went scurrying down a small hill to where a small patch of blue flowers grew. He picked a handful and hurried back to me. "For my old lady, man," he smiled. "You're gonna' like her, Ken. She's a goddamn forest goddess. We found out last week that she's pregnant. Man, ain't that something?" he asked and smiled as broad as the day. "We're gonna' deliver my own kid with only God and the trees looking on!"

I smiled and nodded in agreement, happy to be sharing his joy.

We continued our way along the road for a couple of minutes. Both of us were a little high and feeling at home among the trees. Doc stopped abruptly and with a quick turn of his head, he saw that no one could see us and said, "Come on, man, run!"

In a second, we had both raced across the road and crashed through a thicket and over a broken section of the barbed wire fence that marked the private property of Big Sur. Once out of sight of the road, we began to climb a small hill. Running down from the heights of this particular mountain was a small creek; we jumped it and found ourselves at the foot of a clay cliff. "Yeah, Ken," said Doc with a wink, "we climb." Using roots and vines hanging from the trees above us, we struggled up the cliff and into a small clearing.

The road was far behind and below us; the cliff and the trees completely isolated this clearing. The cool seaside air was a perpetual twilight because the sunlight blocked by the thousands of branches and leaves slowly filtered to the ground, creating a dancing display of sparkling shadows on shadows.

There were a couple of tents, a couple of heavy blankets strung up in temporary lean-tos. A large pile of rocks, set up as a kind of wall, shielded a smoldering campfire that was slowly being stirred by a dark-haired woman.

"Kenny," said Doc, holding out his arms to embrace the clearing, "this is Burgie Burrow! Welcome!"

"Thanks, man," I said, smiling and rubbing the back of my head. "This is really something."

"Kathy!" Doc called out to the woman by the fire. "This is Kenny, a Leo!"

"Far out!" she laughed and came over to where we were standing. "Hi, Kenny. Have you eaten? No one is back yet, but we'll eat in a couple of hours."

"Thanks. Appreciate it," I said, nodding at both Doc and Kathy.

"It's all right, man, we often don't have much, but we generally eat here in the glade." Doc laughed, then turned to Kathy and held out his flowers. "For you, Babe!"

Kathy threw back her head and laughed, her long dark hair falling down to the center of her back. She was dressed in a flowered, embroidered sleeveless smock with tattered jeans and sandals. On one bare arm, she wore a beaded slave bracelet. She took a few of the flowers and stuck them in the bracelet. Then, turning to Doc, she put two in his blond curly hair so they fell over his right ear. Turning to me with the last flower, she gently stuck it in the knot of the red scarf around my neck.

"Thanks again," I laughed as we all sat down by the smoldering fire. "Why did you call this place Burgie Burrow?"

"Well," Doc said, "a guy named Jim Burgie discovered this place. He lives in that first tent over there. He's kind of a weird guy, quiet, you know, but one hell of a tight dude. Anyway, since he found the place, those of us crashing here started calling it Burgie Burrow, kind of thanking him for finding it for us."

"How many people live here?" I asked, toying absently with my leather wrist band.

"I don't know," said Kathy. "Sometimes a lot, other times, just a couple. Crazy Horse, Biker Jim and Burgie have been here the longest."

"Crazy Horse is really something," laughed Doc, slapping his knee. "Crazy is crazy as hell."

"But he's really sweet," Kathy interjected. "I mean, he's a little retarded, but not mean or anything. And if you're his friend and really, truly like him, he'll do anything for you."

"That's for sure," Doc said in a serious tone. "Man, that dude's wild if he thinks anything or anybody's out to hurt a friend of his. I know for a fact he once climbed on top of a pig car with a goddamned club and caved in the windows when the damned cops busted a friend of his."

"I guess he didn't have many friends in school," said Kathy. "You know how cruel children can be. Crazy never even learned to read. He was too busy fighting all the creeps who teased him. He quit before he was even sixteen and hit the road. How old is he now, Doc? Sixteen? Seventeen?"

"Seventeen," Doc said. "Kind of burned out and crazy, but we like him and he likes it here. See over there?" he said, pointing to a hollow tree resting on top of two other fallen giants of the forest. "That's his tree. He lives there. Calls it his first house."

"Biker Jim's something else, too," Doc continued. "He's an ex-biker too, from New York and the Street Commandos. I never heard of 'em, but he says they were a bad bunch. And he's probably right."

"He used to be a speed freak," said Kathy. "And he's still pretty jittery, kind of dangerous. He's got a thing for knives."

"Yeah, but he ain't hurt nobody," said Doc reproachfully. "He's just an old street fighter, and he's been in enough hassles to have reason to be edgy."

"You should talk!" laughed Kathy. "You ain't hardly got any teeth left. Man, did you ever win one?"

"A few," Doc said with a grin and a wink. He slipped his false upper teeth half way out of his mouth in a grotesque joke.

I laughed, knowing what he meant. My mustache hid

several scars on my lips where my teeth had come ripping through the flesh as I tried to prove what a good pacifist I was.

The sun was just going down as Kathy, Doc and I did another number and the other residents of Burgie Burrow returned one by one and began building the evening meal.

All my life, from childhood to the present, one thing I remember is the meals. I remember my father sitting at the head of the family table with me sitting still, afraid to spill a glass of milk for fear of punishment. It was at mealtime that the authority of my parents was confirmed and administered. Punishments for the day's wrong-doings and dark predictions for tomorrow were all meted out at mealtime.

Perhaps it was no accident, then, that since I was fifteen and old enough to support myself, I had been a cook at several restaurants. In a way, the person responsible for the food that others are to eat is both asking and demanding respect. The cook stands away from everyone else, has no direct contact with the customers as do the waitress and waiter. Still, the final authority ("This food is ready to serve.") and the final responsibility ("Take it back, it's not good enough.") rests with the cook.

To some degree, the road to Big Sur and Burgie Burrow was part of a meal ticket I had been riding for many years. In Iowa, months earlier, I had been offered a job as manager of a restaurant with the impressive salary and community status that comes with money. For that job, I'd almost left the streets, but I was a nineteen-year-old drifter, a part of Trans-Amerika and not ready to handle the responsibility. I turned down the job in Iowa, and within a week, I was on the pavement of San Francisco, being fed in the way of the streets--hand to mouth.

In Burgie Burrow, mealtime was a ritual. We gathered together around the blazing campfire and shared our meager resources with each other. A can, a kettle, some rice, a little beef stock, anything any of us had was shared with the others. The meals in the glade meant more than a lot of people eating by a fire. They meant together. All of us were alone, but at night, when we shared our food, we weren't alone any more.

It was my first night in Burgie Burrow. The fire blazed high and gave a strange flickering light to all that surrounded the flames. It was dark, and time to get to know each other by the gentlest means possible--the warmth of a campfire.

I sat shivering slightly in the night's chill, but soon, I found myself smiling, the warmth of the smile started from the inside and worked its way out, making me forget the chill of the seaside evening. I looked across the flames to Doc sitting at the entrance to his tent, softly speaking with Kathy, the fire playing friendly games with their smiles.

I sat there enjoying the company, feeling almost content for a change. As I looked into the fire, flickering and surrounding the branches it was consuming, I heard a voice. "How do, Kenny? Do I got the name right?" It was Biker Jim, leaning above me and holding out his hand. The fire glinted off the knife in his left hand and the ring in his ear. His eyes were somewhat glassy and jittery, but really friendly, as only a campfire in the forest can bring out.

"Yeah, you're right," I said, taking his hand.

"Hey man," said Jim in a soft excited tone, as if we were about to share a great secret. "Have you seen my staff?"

"No, I haven't," I said, feeling confused.

Eager to show a prized possession to the newcomer, he quickly hurried away and came back with his staff.

"Here, man, go ahead, I'll let you hold it. Ain't it something? Man, I did it myself. I'm still working on it, but you can see what it is," said Jim with an excited voice filled with genuine pride in an honest accomplishment.

I held the staff carefully in my hands. He had taken a six foot branch and slowly, carefully, carved into it every symbol that had affected his life.

There were the swastikas and one percenter symbols of his former outlaw days, to the peace symbols and flowers of the calmer life he had found in the mountains. He had spent quite a bit of time with that staff and his knife, creating a small monument to himself out of a piece of wood. In that stick, that piece of the forest, lay an important part of the man, a part of himself he treasured highly and wanted all who knew him to look at and understand.

Jim had very little in the way of property, his knife, the clothes on his back--or at least what sufficed for clothes in Trans-Amerikan poverty--two blankets and his staff, and now he wanted me to share it with him. I could do nothing but take his hand in mine, give him a sincere "Thank you," and be grateful that two people could share the campfire.

Jim and I sat by the fire, saying little, letting the fire carry us to worlds of the mind and our yesterdays. I slowly rolled a joint, hampered a bit by the flickering light, but grinning at the task. I twisted it closed, licked it all over and set it aside to dry as Jim handed me a gallon of cheap wine.

"Here, guy. This is genuine imported rotgut. Bad for what ails 'ya and good for what doesn't," Jim laughed.

"What you say, man?" I laughed and took a long pull on the bottle, then another to wash down the first.

"I don't know, man," Jim answered as we both lost our thoughts in laughter. "Maybe it's imported from L.A."

I lit up the number and sent it following the wine around the circle of fire-lit faces.

In a while, the wine was gone as well as several more numbers and a couple of pipes. The group turned into a laughing, singing insult to every chorus that was ever able to hold a note.

I had claimed and cleaned a large hollow log for my home. It was on the ridge above the campsite and from it I had an almost omniscient view of the fire-lit glade below. Feeling my head spinning with wine, dope and laughter, I asked the bugs sharing my log to please move over for me, and I crawled inside my bedroll. Lulled by the sounds of the forest night, I slept with a peaceful contentment that I had rarely known.

The morning was chilly when I finally decided to crawl out of the warmth of my bedroll. Many of the others were already up and huddled around the fire fixing breakfast. Breakfast wasn't much, just toast, butter and water. But it would sustain us until our evening meal.

After the meal, we crawled down from the mountain to begin our day of scrounging. We were preditors by day and settled down to domesticity in the darkness.

I had always done my own hustling and was fairly good at it. I kept myself well fed most of the time, so now all I had to do was gather a little more for a few extra people. The mountains of Big Sur and the Pacific Ocean provided a peaceful retreat for all who wanted to camp beneath the leaves and beside the sea. All, that is, who were willing to pay. The land of Big Sur is owned, fenced and guarded. Elaborate campsites were erected to offer the monied citizens of Amerika a place to be comfortably rugged. It was in these campsites that I did my hunting.

I walked to the gate and the two people inside the booth. No one who hasn't paid for the privilege to see the trees was allowed past the gate. "How do, folks?" I held in my best good-morning voice. "Have you seen a tall dude, red head band, black hair? I've got to find him."

"No," said one of the men in the booth in a rather suspicious voice. "Why do you want him?"

"He's supposed to be here setting up camp. I had to work last weekend and said I'd meet him here today," I said.

"O.K. You can go look for him," said the man as he adjusted his glasses on the bridge of his nose. Then, leaning over a bit, he added, "Don't be too long."

"Yeah, fine, thanks, man," I said, skipping into the campsite.

As I prowled through the empty trailers and campsites, I hoped no one would return in a hurry and catch me in the act. I wasn't looking for anything big, just a few useful items for our glade. To those who had paid for their campfires, I was, of course, a thief. But to the freaks of Trans-Amerika, I was an outlaw provider.

In one trailer, I found several army mess kits and a fire screen. In another I found a small leather sack filled with orange sunshine acid and half a dozen lids. I didn't take all of it, just a few hits of the acid and one lid.

I returned to the glade with my booty thrown into a sack and stuffed inside my shirt. The sun was still high, but I had been lucky in my scrounging and I decided not to press my luck with any more thefts that day. The fire was a pile of glowing coals when I returned to it; the embers would serve to light the large fire when the others returned.

I sat alone by the smoldering fire and looked up to the trees and the leafy branches. I couldn't see the sun through the leaves, but the hundreds of slivers of light breaking through the forest and lighting the mossy ground with a million patches of sun and shadow were far more beautiful. The soft forest carpet I sat on was so soft I felt like I would sink into its living fibre. I was relaxed. My mind was wandering back to times of long ago.

I could remember jail cells, court rooms, miles of highway covered with snow and racked by bitter cold winds, nights of

passion in a sleeping bag or a bed. I remembered throwing
my packs on my shoulders and walking out a door. I had
turned to say one thing more and found the door shut behind
me. Perhaps she didn't want to hear any more, or perhaps
she didn't know I had any more to say. For whatever reason,
she had shut the door.

Now I was sitting by a nearly dead fire, admiring the
leaves and sunlight. Here, in the forest, the tears I had
refused to shed and spill on the pavement of any city or let
any citizen of Amerika see, seemed to well up in my eyes. I
lay back on the moss and holding back the tears once more, I
found myself smiling as Crazy Horse approached me.

With an almost shy wave of his hand, he greeted me. His
coarse brown hair hung in greasy curls to his shoulders. He
wore a leather head hand studded with gold stars and
adorned with one red feather hanging next to his cheek. His
shirt was a tattered remnant of a classic cowboy shirt, and he
wore one pair of torn jeans over another. Swaying a bit and
holding a half gallon of wine, he joined me on the mossy
forest floor.

"How do, dude? What's happening, man?" he said,
handing me the wine.

"Just brought in a few possibles for the group," I said,
pointing to the sack of spoils by the fire.

"That's cool, Kenny," he said. "Hey, man, ain't this
place somethin'? Christ, it's beautiful, trees and all. Have
you seen my house? A whole log for my house. Ain't that
somethin'?"

"Yeah, Crazy, that's really something. I like my log too.
It's not as good as yours, but they're both home," I said as I
began to roll a number.

"Hey, Kenny, have you been swimming yet?" asked
Crazy.

"You mean at the gorge?" I asked. "No, I haven't."

About five miles from our section of forest was the gorge,
a communal swimming hole for all the people of
Trans-Amerika. Crazy and I nodded to each other and started
walking.

"You know, Kenny," said Crazy Horse. "I'm from
Kansas, Wichita. Man, like that's one screwed up place. The
teacher used to make me stand in front of the room and read
out loud because I was the worst reader."

"Was she being mean, man, or what?" I asked.

"Well, the bitch said that public exposure would help me read better. Shit, I'd stand up there and all the rest of those assholes whould laugh at me and throw pennies and stuff. One day, I got pissed and started crying. Then everybody started laughing even more. Then I hit one bastard with my book. Broke his nose, I guess. So they kicked me out. Man, my old man beat the living Christmas out of me for it, so while everyone else was asleep, I left. Even ripped off the old man for more than a hundred bucks."

"Haven't been back again, Crazy?" I asked as we stopped for a second and lit the number.

"Naw, I hated the place. Mmmm, that's good. Thanks, man," he said, accepting the joint and taking a deep hit.

"Don't you miss anything about the place? I mean, like it was home once," I said.

"Yeah, one chick," he said. "I really loved her. She never laughed at me. She had a horse and we used to go riding and stuff. Someday, I'm going back there and take her with me. Shit, man," he sighed. "The last time her dad saw me with her, he said he'd bust me for rape because she was only fifteen. But, shit, I was barely sixteen."

I nodded my head having nothing to add to what the guy had said. "Hey, Crazy, hey dude," I said slapping him on his stooped shoulders, "have a hit, man. Let's get loaded and go swimming."

He looked at me and smiled slightly, taking the joint from me and took a long pull that nearly finished the thing. Silently we walked along the forest path. Suddenly, he turned to me. "Kenny, will you be my friend?"

I looked at him, his eyes shining from his smoke-soiled face, filled with tears and hope. I laughed, not an insulting laugh, but one of surprise. "Crazy, you beautiful nut, we already are!"

With a joyous whoop, he began to laugh, and soon we were both running, laughing and singing our way along the forest trail toward the gorge and an afternoon swim.

Crazy Horse and I stood beneath a large tree watching the other swimmers. In a second, he was naked except for his headband and happily splashing in the water. I undressed slowly, marveling at the beauty of the scene.

A rather large creek flowed down the mountains and off a

cliff creating a dazzling waterfall. The fall became a pool completely lined by rocks and filled with crystal clear, icy water. About twenty more people were enjoying themselves at the gorge, splashing in the water or lying on the rocks, unashamed in their nakedness.

I smiled, remembering city pools filled with chlorine and people in tight swimsuits, all trying to display their bodies without revealing themselves. Padded tops or bulging jock straps were out of place in this water.

I dove into the water, deep water, clear and icy cold as the mountain stream it was part of. The other diving, swimming bodies made the water churn as all the swimmers became a part of an underwater game, rolling and throwing a small rubber ball to each other and having the ball and its owner lost in a tangled sea of wet bodies.

We swam and laughed for a couple of hours, but when I saw that the sun was going down, I knew it was time to leave.

The return walk was a peaceful stroll through the forest, a kind of relaxing walk that is hard to find on city streets. The light was growing dim and the shadows of trees and branches were beginning to take on fantastic forms. By the time we reached our destination, the twilight shadows were almost gone, and the night was upon us.

The cheery "Hellos" of the other forest people made us feel happy to be home and among them. Several people were already fixing dinner on the liberated utensils and the fire was blazing merrily away, giving a flickering light to the preparation of the meal. The food smelled good and I was hungry, as I figured everyone else was. We sat down around the fire and ate our meal. We shared our stories of Trans-Amerika and how each had arrived at Burgie Burrow. The wine bottles were opened and a few joints rolled. We stoked the fire, laid back, relaxed and content with our own company.

I was just taking a long drink from my canteen when Biker Jim's turn at the conversation caught my attention. "Yeah, I miss it," he was saying to Doc in particular and everyone in general. "I do miss my chop and what it feels like to be riding with fifty of your brothers in formation."

"I can dig that," Doc answered in a low tone as he carefully filled a corn cob pipe with pot. "But the rest of it gets pretty bad sometimes, Jim. Well, you know what I mean. The beatings, the busts, not being able to just sit down with your old lady and dig each other without a half dozen bikers partying around you or a hundred cops crashing through the front door.''

''That's what I mean, man, that's what I was getting at,'' Jim answered after taking a long pull at the wine bottle. ''Here it's calm, peaceful, ya know? Like I'm not constantly looking over my shoulder or sleeping with a gun next to me. I miss part of the vavoom scene, but not all of it by any means. Like I just met Kenny there,'' he said throwing a thumb in my direction. ''And I'm not afraid. He's just like me and you and Crazy and Burgie and all of us, just trying to relax. That's what I mean, man. Here we can calm down, relax and really love each other. Right bro?'' he laughed handing me the wine.

''Yeah, right, dude,'' I said. ''Don't worry, man. I'm not afraid of you either.''

''O.K., then,'' said Doc. ''O.K., none of us want to do anything but live in these mountains, right?'' While we all murmured our assent, he leaned over and lit the pipe. Taking a long hit, he passed it on to Burgie. ''Then why don't we just all stick together and get to know each other? Kind of a family. We don't need nobody else out there, right?''

''What about the winter?'' asked Jim Burgie in a tight voice, his lungs filled with smoke.

''Shit, man'' interrupted Biker Jim, ''we've got about four months to get ready if things are cool and we just start climbing back into these hills. Build homes and live. No one's going to bug us back there.''

''We could raise the kid back there,'' smiled Kathy in a quiet voice as she laid her head on Doc's arm.

I smiled to myself and everyone else as I took my turn on the pipe.

The night drifted slowly through each of us as we discussed our future together. Before this, we had not talked of the future because we felt we had none. This night, there was a kind of closeness that most people, caught up in the mainstream of Amerikan life, are incapable of feeling. It was a sort of childhood revival, reminiscent of times we would gather in a basement or attic to discuss our various stories and misconceptions about sex. A closeness that forbade entrance to any but those already together. A closeness that is somehow lost in the growth of the individual in an impersonal world. We spent the rest of the night softly talking, drinking, smoking and planning how to make our glade into a real communal home.

I woke early in the morning, a little spaced out by the dope and wine, but excited about what the day would bring. Around our breakfast fire, we decided on a real feast to celebrate our birth as a family. In order to have a real family feast, we needed a table to fit our new status...and a good deal of food.

Like a pack of scavengers, we began to prowl the stores and campsites of Big Sur. Biker Jim, Doc and I walked into Big Sur's grocery store. I walked slowly by the canned food section, quickly liberating a few cans of tuna and beans. I came to the frozen meat department and looked at the assortment of meat and poultry, and as I did, I gave a small nod to Doc, who was standing near Biker Jim by a rack of potato chips.

"Mother jumping ape!" Doc screamed at Jim, who immediately answered with a haymaker that sent Doc crashing through the chips and cans and in a second, both men were sending produce flying as they wrestled each other on the floor.

The whole staff of the store jumped in to break up the fray. Taking advantage of the diversion, I quickly skipped out the door with a chicken under my shirt and a good deal of fruit in the pockets of my leather jacket.

Laughing with each other back in the camp, we stashed the food and went out in search of a table top. In one of the straight campsites was a shower building a bit set off from the rest of the camp and shielded by two large trees. With Jim and I standing watch, Doc quickly unscrewed the half dozen bolts holding the door on and let it fall to the ground.

While I talked and argued with the grounds manager about the unfairness of charging money for camping among nature's trees, Doc and Jim slipped silently through the trees and bushes with the door.

By the time we got to our own camp, Jim, Burgie, Kathy, Crazy and the others had already arrived and brought wine and a dozen ears of corn with them.

In the early hours of the evening, we gathered to build our table and prepare our celebration feast. Smiling and laughing, we broke out the dope and wine as Crazy and Kathy barbecued the chicken and roasted the corn.

"Hey, everyone!" shouted Burgie as he finished a long draught of wine. "If we're really free, then what the hell do we want with this motherjumping country?"

Not one of us had an answer for him because we all knew he was right. We looked to him as he stood by the fire and grinned at us, clutching the wine bottle in his hand. He was right, but we couldn't think of any way to let the world know that Burgie Burrow was no longer a part of Amerika.

Crazy, good-hearted, weird Crazy Horse, solved our problem. He hurried back to his hollow log and returned with a large silk flag. "We need our own flag!" he laughed. "A flag of Burgie Burrow. Let's change this mother!"

Laughing and singing, we all gathered around the table and began to work on "old gory" to change it to our own flag. I sacrificed a shirt, bright blue, and we cut a symbol of a mountain from it, sewing the mountain onto the stars of Amerika's flag. On the mountain, we sewed a cannibas leaf and flower symbol. We had our flag and soon it was proudly waving from atop a small pine tree. Cheering like a bunch of freshmen at homecoming game, we saluted our flag.

The next thing we decided to do was to officially withdraw from Amerika. To do this, we wrote a telegram and pooled enough money to send it off the next day:

Richard M. Nixon
President, U.S.A.
1600 Pennsylvania Avenue
Washington, D.C.
Dear Sir:
    You have drafted and killed us, chased us and ignored us. So we are leaving. You can keep your country and your wars. Burgie Burrow has seceded from the Union!

We had left Amerika and liberated our mountain. We were out. We had escaped.

FREE

The darkness of the forest night covered the trees and was broken only by the light of our campfire. We were celebrating our birth as a family, and I decided to drop one of the hits of acid I had come up with earlier.

The fire burned brightly and played strange games with my eyes. Each flame stretched to the tree tops and engulfed the entire forest before becoming a part of the hovering mass of light that watched the group around the fire. I was doing fine. It looked like a very good journey, a fine trip. The night was cool, and the fire was warm and friendly. I looked around at the circle of faces and smiled to myself feeling warm and comfortable with my new family.

Helping us celebrate the evening was a group of about ten guests who were sharing our glade, wine, dope and fire. I gazed at the ring of faces; Crazy idly drumming out a rhythm on the side on an empty wine bottle; Burgie lying back on a log, his long blond hair falling around his shoulders and trembling as if alive when he took a long pull on Doc's corncob pipe. With a warm feeling inside, I lay back on the damp moss-covered ground and let the acid crawl deep into my brain and play games with reality.

"You fucking son of a bitch! I'll kill you!"

I jumped up, shocked, and ran toward the sound. I found Biker Jim squared off, knife in hand with one of the guests. I hurriedly threw a body block into Jim as Doc and Crazy landed on the guest.

Jim and I rolled on the ground, snapping twigs and branches beneath us. He came out on top,.and I saw his eyes full of hate and tears. His cheeks were glistening with wetness. Knife still in hand, he looked down at me as I lay there. He saw that it was I he had pinned to the ground and quickly let me up. Once we were standing, the hardened street fighter turned to me and with a tear-choked voice said, "That motherfucker burned my staff! He broke it and threw the thing into the fire! He burned it, Kenny. He burned my goddamned staff!''

I might have laughed but for Jim's face. Here was a grown man ready to kill another over a piece of wood. But it meant more to him than a piece of wood. Even so, I couldn't see killing someone over it. The stranger made a mistake by burning the staff, and he could easily have died for it.

The stranger turned to Doc and with a trembling voice said, ''I'm sorry! I didn't know! Christ, I thought it was a piece of wood! I really didn't know, honest!''

''It's cool, dude. Don't worry,'' said Doc. ''Have a drink, relax, but kind of stay out of Jim's way tonight, O.K.?''

''Yeah, man, sure. Thanks a lot, you guys,'' the stranger said and sat as far from Jim as he could manage, saying little for the rest of the night. Jim had returned to the fire and was silently sipping a beer.

I staggered back to the fire and fell to my knees, my mind reeling with visions of death and violence. Colors and lights intensified by the fire I was staring into came crashing into my mind. I looked over to the stranger who was still trembling, matches in hand, trying to light a cigarette. In the straight world, value was marked with a price tag, and it's destruction was easily paid for. But the invisible value a lonely man put on a piece of carved wood could have cost someone's life. I trembled at the thought of death in our new home.

Jim sat silently, looking into the fire, his face like iron, the face of a hard, battle-scarred veteran of the streets. With hollow eyes, he looked over at me. Seeing that I was alone, he came over and sat next to me and handed his beer to me. ''Sorry if I hurt ya, man. I didn't know it was you, Kenny,'' he mumbled.

''Don't worry, it's fine,'' I answered.

We said little else. He sharpened his knife and I played color games with the fire. The acid was doing fine, but the visions of blood made me fear losing control of the trip.

It was a strange trip, a weird night with everyone's mind going different directions. As I sat there lost in my own world, I turned back to the group around the fire, curious about their conversations.

Two Jesus freaks, or as they preferred to be called, Christians, were staying with us that night and the idle conversation soon turned to god.

"Jesus is it, man. There isn't any other way. No salvation, no life, nothin' at all without Him," said the one called Brother Michael.

His partner, called Brother Samuel, joined in, "Everyone needs God in his life. People just can't live on their own. They need their Lord."

Their eyes glowed with other-worldly light that those caught up in the fervor of a belief are prone to have. Christians, Followers of Islam, Communists, Buddhists and all the rest share at least that one thing. My eyes, in turn, were glowing with the light of lysergic acid as I said, "True, I don't think that people are alone in this life, but I just can't believe in a god that creates people just to burn them forever in a hell He created just for that purpose."

"But God loves you, man," said Michael. "He sent His son to save you from that hell. All you've got to do is believe in Christ, and you'll never have to fear hell."

"And if I don't believe?" I asked.

"Then you're damning yourself. God's given you a way out. You ignore God and His gift to you, then you've got no one to blame but yourself for your damnation."

"Oh," I muttered giving up the argument before it could really begin. If I were to argue religion from a base of logic and reason, then they would counter with their own brand of logic, based on blind faith. There is no way anyone can argue with faith, so I just smiled at them across the fire.

Kathy leaned closer to the fire, and in a low voice said, "This place here," and she opened her arms to include all of us and our glade, "Burgie Burrow needs God. Maybe not your religion, but at least some sort of god to watch over us."

As she spoke, I watched her through my acid haze, and she turned into a soft, gentle wood nymph, a symbol of freedom in the forest.

"I mean," she continued, "we've got nothing to hang onto except each other, and like you said, it ain't enough. Even Ken would agree to that much."

I looked up and nodded, then returned to the night time hallucinations of my trip.

Doc surprised me by turning to Samuel. "Would you like to lead us in a short prayer? It can't hurt and it might help," he said.

So together we bowed our heads in prayer and hope. I too joined in the prayer to a nonexistent god. I had been to church many years earlier but not since. I wasn't sure why I was bowing my head now. Perhaps in a desperate hope that there was a god up there who knew me and loved me.

I thought of my father, who had always professed his atheism. But when his mother died, I saw that stubborn atheist go down on his knees and pray. At the time I had scorned his weakness. But now, here on this mountain by the fire, I too was praying. For a time, both of us had lost our grip on reality, a grip that was none too strong to begin with, and reached out in desperation to something beyond reality. I found I could not scorn another man's weakness without recognizing my own.

The final words of the prayers were echoing through my head"...please, Lord, keep these people in this place safe from harm...In Jesus' name we ask it. Amen..." when I heard a bull horn shatter the peaceful night.

"All right! Douse that fire!"

We panicked. "Rangers! On the road!"

The fire was quickly put out, and Doc and Burgie hurried along down the mountain to check it out. Biker Jim, Crazy Horse and I crouched on a boulder, knives drawn, ready for battle.

All was dark. The only light we had, the campfire, was out and there was no way to see the moon or stars through the thick branches. My mind was reeling because I couldn't tell light from dark in the drug maze inside my head. I crawled farther onto the boulder, imagining an attack of armed rangers on this mountain.

I knew I could kill someone to defend my right to live in this forest. I heard voices all around me as the others prepared to defend their home. I turned to Jim, but all I could see were his eyes as they glowed catlike in the night. I knew his blade was ready and that he knew how to use it. I suddenly felt like jumping off the boulder and crawling beneath it for the duration of the struggle. With my mind changing and flashing as it was, there would be no way for me to tell friend from foe in a fight.

There were voices all around me, and I couldn't tell what they were saying or whose they were. But I stayed there, sweat pouring from my face, my body tense and still, ready to strike at anyone who touched me.

My eyes burned for a second as I saw a flash to my right, the momentary flash became a small, bright flame, and I heard Doc laugh.

"It's O.K., group. Everything's fine. The rangers just popped some dudes who were camping by the road. Nobody's coming up here."

I sat down on a boulder, my chest heaving with my gasping breath, my body tense for fighting collapsed into itself. I sat there alone, trembling and shaking as the fire was rekindled and everyone gathered around it, laughing at the experience, at their own panic and fear.

My mind was reeling with visions and reflections of blood, prayer, lights and rangers' faces, all reflected in the fire. The whole collage of sights and sounds seemed ready to cave in and burst in a screaming explosion inside my head. I could hardly move or feel my body as I sat alone, trying to regain control of my thoughts. Having nothing to say to anyone, I crawled off to my log to try to sleep and come down.

I slept. A fitful night, broken by dreams of myself floating amid the dreams of the Burgie Burrow family. We were together, defending each other, smiling at one another over our meals and swimming beneath the falls. The hopes and dreams that were now centered around this mountain retreat came to life as the children of a fear-filled mind.

I woke late that morning. It had taken a long time to come down from the swirling visions in my mind to whatever sense of reality I could find. I could hear the sounds of a guitar and mouth harp gently working to wake everyone up for breakfast.

Doc and Kathy sat in their tent making pleasant music for all to start the day with. I opened my eyes wide to look at the green of our glade and the beauty of the morning contrasting with the fear of the previous night.

So I smiled at the trees and listened for a moment to the gentle sounds of our soft-running stream. I rose and slowly walked to the fire and a family breakfast.

When human beings feel close to each other, they share food. Weddings, funerals, parties, seductions, Bar Mitzvas, graduations, all are marked with the symbolic act of eating together. Our family too shared closeness by sharing food.

EXIT

I walked slowly along the road, Hippie Highway 101, kicking a smooth pebble in front of me. I looked at the rows of thumbers trying to leave Big Sur and continue their lives in Trans-Amerika. They were holding signs announcing their destinations: every place from Mexico to New York. A lot of people on the road with places they felt they needed to go, destinations.

I turned off the road and walked toward the ocean. I needed to listen to the waves for awhile.

I'd been living in the mountains now for almost two weeks. I loved my woodland family, loved them so much I often felt I could cry. But still, there was a gnawing inside me that prevented me from being completely at peace in the forest.

I sat down on the beach. It wasn't really a beach, just a rocky shoreline, but for now it was the only beach I had. I leaned back against a tree and looked up to its leafy branches and listened to the waves as one by one they came to the shore.

I was tired. Not physically tired, but feeling the weariness caused by trying to carry a heavy, unknown weight inside. The waves rolled in and shattered themselves on the rocks, then rolled back to the sea. I closed my eyes and lay back listening to the sounds of waves. They came from far away, made a brief visit ten feet from my inert body and then returned to far, far away.

I remembered what someone said about me once and smiled. "Some people burn their bridges behind them. Some people burn bridges to keep from crossing them...Kenny burns his bridges, then tries to cross them."

Here I was on the shores of the Pacific trying to remember a past I could never see again. Admiring, or at least listening to the waves on this shore, coming from somewhere and returning somewhere. I had come from somewhere once, but I knew I couldn't return. I too was paying a visit to this shore, but unlike the waves, it looked as if I would remain.

I thought of the other people at Burgie Burrow...Biker Jim was busily carving a new staff for himself, eagerly telling of the snakes and crosses that he would carve into it. Doc woke that morning hurting. The cold dampness of the mountains sometimes made his leg stiffen and pain him. Kathy hadn't felt any too well herself, she claimed morning sickness.

Kathy and I had talked for awhile that morning about her child. "It really is beautiful here, Kenny," she had said. "We lived in cities for so long, ya know, and we almost forgot how beautiful trees can be. But our baby won't forget. If I have my way, our child will always live in the forest. Here you can breath and feel grass while you walk, not concrete. Man, smog, buildings and parking lots ain't no way to grow up. Our baby's going to be raised where it's soft and natural. Not cold, mean and artificial."

There was nothing for me to say to her. All I could do was try to give a reassuring smile, all the while looking to the time when smog and pavement would run over the Big Sur mountains.

As I was prowling the campsites of the citizens of Amerika that morning, I had stopped to watch a prediction of Amerika's future. A truck from a nearby fish hatchery was parked on a small bridge over a stream. Two men were throwing hundreds of trout into the stream. Not more than ten feet from the bridge, a line of people gathered. The line stretched for as far as I could see. A line of human beings, each armed with a rod and reel, eagerly hooking the fish as they swam by.

I looked at the truck, then at the fish. I looked at the fishermen and then back to the fish. Back to the truck, then back to the fishermen and I started to laugh. I must have stood there for couple of minutes, laughing like a fool.

Here we were, living in the great Amerikan wilderness, being spoon fed fish from a hatchery truck. Here I was, attempting to escape that same civilization that produced the truck and sportsmen with their rods and reels by feeding myself and others by preying on the same sportsmen I was laughing at.

I opened my eyes and thought again of Kathy's baby. I guess she and I both knew that her child would see more smog and pavement than trees and flowers.

I watched the waves some more. They were so fine, so permanent and regular. They were almost like the heartbeat of the earth. I wondered how a child felt when it suckled at its mother's breast and listening to her regular, permanent heartbeat. I wondered if that was what I felt when I came to the shore, and if that's what everyone seeks when they turn to the sea.

Soon I was walking again, back toward the highway and back to the mountain. As I crossed the highway, I saw a sign held by a thumber headed toward Cleveland. The thumber, a young woman with long, dark hair tied in a braid and hanging over one shoulder, smiled at me and motioned for me to sit down.

"How do," I said. "So what's in Cleveland?" I sat down beside her.

"A place to live for awhile," she said with light grin. She lit a number and handed it to me. As we shared the joint, we carried on one of those meaningless conversations about highways, dope, booze and places we both had been.

As we finished the weed, I asked her why she was leaving the beauty of the mountains and going back to the grime and hustle of the city.

"Well," she said, tossing her long braid over her other shoulder, "I can't stay here forever, you know."

"Why not?" I asked, confused.

"Kenny," she said, "This place is a vacation from a lot of things for a lot of people. Some pay money; some, like you and I, don't. But there's really no difference. It's still just a vacation. If you really want to live, you go to where life is. And in this society, that's in the cities and towns. If you need a rest, you come here, to the ocean, for awhile. But if you try to stay here or any place like this forever, then you're giving up the struggle of life. If you give up that struggle, you're as good as dead. I don't know about you, but my vacation is over. I'm nineteen years old and not ready to die."

I looked at her and shook my head. Maybe she was right, who knows? I had intended to invite her back to Burgie Burrow, but our forest retreat, our flag had nothing for her. I smiled, embraced her and said, "Well, have a good life in Cleveland."

She turned to me, handed me a piece of paper with an

address on it and said, "If you want to leave, I'll be here in a week."

I thanked her, accepted the sheet of paper and headed toward my mountain. As I began to climb, I looked back to the road as a truck stopped and picked her up. I turned away and continued my climb.

I entered the glade a little early. Very few people were there yet, but sitting outside his log house was Crazy Horse with a bottle of wine. He called me over to share the wine. So we sat in the grass and drank the wine, talking of Burgie Burrow.

"You know, man," he said, "I really feel nice here. Like nobody hassles you here, man. They let you live, really they do. Man, my old man used to kick the shit out of me just because I couldn't read or spell right. Like is that any way to be. Huh, is it?" He raised his arms to embrace the entire camp.

"Shit, man, like this is my home now. I'm never going to go back to that again. I'll just live here, maybe build a cabin. I know how to build a cabin. I really do," he finished, eyes glowing.

I took a light drink of the wine and thought back to the conversation I'd had on the road a few minutes earlier. She was leaving the forest to live and Crazy Horse was living here. Myself, I didn't know. I had nothing to return to, so I was here drinking wine and listening to Crazy Horse.

Crazy looked at me with a kind of trembling voice and tear-filled eyes. "I'm glad you're here, Kenny. I love you," he said.

To that there was nothing to say, nothing at all. I looked at him and silently handed him the wine.

Later, as we sat around dinner together talking about our many collective yesterdays and tomorrows, I was silent. I was thinking about the fishermen that afternoon, thinking about the pavement. We were here sitting on the grass and moss trying to run from the pavement. I guess I knew that pavement would catch up to the grass and moss someday. When that happened, we would be doled out our allotment of greenery the same as the fish that were dumped into the stream.

I knew my time at Burgie Burrow was over. I too was nineteen years old and very much alive. I couldn't stay on a mountain forever. I turned from the fire and sat beneath a tree away from the light.

In the dark I watched the others around the campfire. Biker Jim sat away from the others, knife in hand, busily working on his new staff. All the others were turned to Doc and Kathy, who were playing a long, sad song for everyone.

At that moment, I loved every member of that small community of people. The music of Doc's mouth harp and Kathy's guitar brought everyone together, and I loved them all.

I looked up, straining to see the flag in the dark. I failed, but I knew it was there above us all. I remembered our message to the President, and I knew I was a part of these people and this place. And they would always be a part of me. We had all been driven to this mountain. I didn't know if the others would ever leave, but I knew I had to. I didn't know where, but I knew I couldn't stay there any longer.

Doc's leg was stretched out in front of him, a bit swollen with pain. Doc was twenty six and looked at least forty. His teeth were gone, lost in a hundred fights, and his eyes had the look of an old prospector living and hiding in the mountains because he didn't know any place else to search for his treasures. Doc looked at me, smiled, waved me over and handed me a bottle of wine. I took a drink and passed the bottle.

Around my neck were two strings of beads. One had been given to me a year earlier as I was passing through South Dakota. The other was a product of my own hands. I took the second string from my neck and turned to Doc. I couldn't say anything. I felt a lot of things deep in my heart, but I had no words to use.

I looked at Doc and said, "Here. Thank you."

He looked back at me, took the beads and slowly put them around his neck. Then he did something unexpected. He leaned over and embraced me, warmly, strongly.

I left the fire and returned to by bedroll for my last night's sleep in Burgie Burrow.

I woke from my sleeping place and watched the beginnings of the morning meal's ritual. This morning was different because I was leaving. Because I was going to go, I felt I couldn't sit with the others or even share their food for the final time.

Instead, I methodically gathered up my gear and tried not to look at anyone. My pack, bedroll, knife and various odds and ends were soon in order. I was ready to leave.

I began my last climb down the mountain without saying goodbye. I didn't know why, but it just wasn't inside me to attempt farewells. I turned and waved. No one spoke a word in the forest. They simply looked at me. Doc stiffly got to his feet and waved. I smiled, turned away, and started down the slope.

I reached 101 and sat down, wondering which way to go. I looked back up the mountain, but I couldn't see the flag. It didn't really matter. I knew it was there, the same I knew who was there.

The first car to come along was going north, so I was going north too. Once again, I was just another Trans-Amerikan freak, going nowhere special, simply going, on the move. A couple of hours later, I was in Carmel.

I could see the buildings of the city and hear the cars on the highway, but the ocean and the forest were too far away to see or hear now.

I went into the men's room at a service station and looked at myself in the mirror. The reflection was a person I didn't know. The face reflected was covered with dirt and smoke. The hair was dark and matted, the teeth were yellow and gray. The eyes were deep, bloodshot, sad. As I saw myself, I suddenly felt filthy. A closer examination of the hair revealed a few stray lice. I stripped to the waist and began to scrub myself furiously.

Then, deciding to do something about the unwelcomed guests in my hair, I left the men's room and approached the attendant. He was a smiling kid of about sixteen, leaning against a fuel pump, eating an apple he sprinkled with salt.

"Hey, man," I mumbled, "can I buy a quart of gas?"

"Sure thing," he said, "glad to help. He put a bit of fuel in a can and handed it to me.

"Can I bum that salt, too?" I asked, pointing to the salt shaker.

"Sure, man," he laughed. "What are these for anyway?"

"Well, cleanliness is next to Fordliness," I laughed.

For the next half hour I scrubbed my scalp with the gasoline and then with the strong gas station soap. I scrubbed my teeth with the salt until they were at least semi-white. After scrubbing my whole body and changing into clean clothes, I shouldered my gear and left the service station. Thanking the attendant, I skipped into town.

The next couple of hours, I walked along the sidewalks, smiling at the friendliest looking people with my greeting of, "Got any spare change?"

After I'd hustled a couple of bucks, I made my way back to the highway, stopping for a moment again at the service station. The attendant just finished filling a car.

"Getting busier, I see," and I smiled.

"Gonna' get busier than this before the day's over," he answered. "Today, they'll bust my ass for sure."

"How come?" I asked.

"Today's a holiday, everybody's traveling, and they need the gas," he replied.

"Holiday?" I asked, surprised, "What holiday?"

"Man, where you been? Today's the Fourth of July!" he laughed.

"Independence Day, huh?" I grinned and scratched my head. "Well, that's far out."

Waving goodbye, I headed for 101 north. As I sat there, I stared back down the road toward the Big Sur mountains, remembering a place, thinking fondly of a group of people I somehow knew I'd never see again.

PART II

TRAVELING MUSIC

"Twilight reflections
broken by the street lights,
beckoning the traveler
to sin. . ."

Lyftogt

FREAK HOLIDAY

I closed my eyes, feeling a wave of sensation rising through my body and sending my head spinning through space. Gasping in breathless wonder, I opened my eyes again and looked around me. The sun was high and beating down on me as I sat on the hood of a parked car. My first ride out of Carmel had given me a hit of acid. It was supposed to be psilocybin, but I would bet there wasn't a trace of mushroom in it. It was, however, fine righteous acid, and I didn't much mind the deception. I closed my eyes again as another exciting acid rush came roaring through my body sending me flying through time and distance.

The car I was sitting on was one of the hundreds of cars caught in a traffic jam in Santa Cruz. Again, I opened my eyes to survey the sight. It was the Fourth of July, a holiday, and all of Amerika seemed to be on the move. The shaggy freaks of Trans-Amerika seemed to be out in full strength too. Vans, old paint-peeling cars, hearses and station wagons all filled with laughing people going nowhere in the jam, but enjoying each others company under the hot summer sky.

I took a deep hit from the number I was holding and passed it to a smiling stranger who was leaning against the car. The straight people of Amerika looked on with disapproval as we smoked our dope. But since quite a few of them had broken into their coolers for an illicit beer or two before driving on, they did nothing. In a holiday crowd like this, freaks could freely smoke their weed because Amerikan police were too busy directing traffic to bust anyone for anything.

I was stoned, flying higher every moment and digging the Independence Day crowd. A dude named Eric owned the car I was on. He had picked me up an hour or so earlier. Now, in the jam we sat on the car passing joints, sharing the freak holiday.

Eric laughed and handed a joint to some black dudes in a nearby car. They in turn handed him a bottle of wine. Laughing came easily for Eric. To him the world was simply a showcase for laughs. He had been a part of Trans-Amerika for a long time; a vegetarian, alcoholic, acid-head freak with three years growth of hair that he refused to wash or comb. He wore a battered straw cowboy hat on top of the matted blonde hair and two bright blue eyes glowed from behind his sun-burned face. Beneath his long, hooked nose drooped a straggly mustache.

He laughed again and handed me the wine. Eric was strange. To him, everything that could be was, and things generally thought of as impossible became incredibly real in his mind. I took a long pull on the wine and laughed with Eric.

I turned my head as I heard a noise like a swarm of gigantic bees. They came, one by one, grinding low in first gear. Outlaw bikers, considered by many to be the psychedelic storm troopers of Trans-Amerika, but in reality they were a breed totally their own. They were a wild, vicious element who claimed no kin in either the world of freaks or straights.

I watched silently as they came, walking their chops through the maze of cars in the traffic jam. There seemed to be hundreds of them, dressed in sleeveless denim and leather jackets. Long hair, leather gloves, drive chains for belts, 1% symbols and their patches, which read "Gypsy Jokers" and "Madcaps." Two outlaw clubs on a holiday run to Santa Cruz.

I watched them with a strange mixture of fear and respect. They didn't have to wait on a highway for a generous person to pick them up. They rode their machines anyplace and anytime they wanted to, free of the opinions of anyone. Underneath the freedom, below the joy of movement, was a seething violence that could explode at any moment and leave a bloody tribute to their passing. I watched the outlaws, but I kept a respectful distance.

But now I was flying, screaming high on the day, acid rushing me upward in a traffic jam, dope being smoked and passed on, wine wetting thirsty throats, the hot sun high above shining down on the holiday. I didn't want to ever lose this high. I didn't want to come down for anything. Eric looked over to a big biker who was idling his chop next to us. Eric broke into a toothy smile and handed him the wine. With a flourish, the biker finished the wine and threw the bottle into the back seat of a convertable, grinning in challenge at the nervous faces of the two passengers. I laughed, not caring. There were bikers all around, some trying to direct traffic, others jostling and partying with each other in the traffic jam.

After a while the streets cleared up a bit and we slowly started to move. The acid was doing me fine as we crept through the streets of Santa Cruz; colors, people, machines and buildings melting and running before my eyes. It was Independence Day, and I felt it. I had my packs, a few dollars, a little dope and I was loaded. No one I met knew me, I just threw my packs into their cars. They read "Trans-Amerika" and knew all they needed to know.

I lay my head back on the car seat, the acid flashing highway memories before me. I had taken my first look at California two years earlier and also my first acid trip in a small apartment in L.A. Somehow, later, I had managed to finish my tour of duty in high school, stoned most of the time. I was on the move the morning after I'd stood on a stage in my cap and gown, raising a clenched fist. I wasn't sure how it all began..the beat of a rock band, a flower I handed a stranger on the street, a book about Robin Hood. Somehow it began, and now it was me, riding in a car on the Fourth of July.

My mind was spiraling upward like Dorothy's house on its way to Oz as Eric and I came to a door. There was a party going on inside. A fine stereo was blasting out solid rock music, and I immediately found myself an empty corner to sit in. There were two couples dancing, a few more sitting around a large water pipe, and a woman sitting alone on a bed playing an acoustic guitar, her notes drowned by the electronic, amplified music from the stereo.

"That's Kenny over there," I heard someone say. I had heard it before, often. In a hundred places over thousands of miles the same questions came up. "Who's that sleeping on the floor?" "Is he nice?" "Who's that over there?" Always I could give one answer, "I'm Kenny."

"Yeah, I'm Kenny," I thought to myself as I enjoyed the party from the sanctuary of my corner. "Not a soul here knows me and that's the way it should be. As long as we're happy, I can come or go and nobody's going to be hurt."

"Hey, Ken, do you need some coin?" someone asked.

"Huh, what?" I started, brought out of the clouds of my thoughts by Eric's voice as he handed me a beer.

"Do you need some money, man?" he repeated.

"Yeah, thanks man, I'm broke," I muttered in a confused voice not understanding what he was saying. "Hey, hold it man, I'm mixed up, I'm wrecked out of my skull so please, go through it again, slowly. Why would you give me money?" I continued.

With a light laugh he said "OK fella, one more time. These guys here are in a band and have a gig in Palo Alto tonight, I'm their road manager, and I could use some help setting things up. So if you want I'll give you five and a place to crash for awhile. It ain't much but it's more than you're making now."

I took a drink of my beer and nodded my head and said, "Thanks a lot. Sure I'll do it."

"Great!" laughed Eric. "Hey group, Ken said he'd join our motley crew for awhile!"

His announcement was greeted with a happy cheer and an impromptu toast of wine glasses, beer bottles and dope pipes.

"Oh, wow!" I exclaimed to myself as the toast brought on a tremendous acid rush that threatened to send my brain into a distant never never land of stars and blazing colors. I felt my mind moving inside itself, agitated and vibrating inside the shell of my skull, it cried out for freedom.

"Hey man," I said to Eric, "how long before we get going?"

"An hour or so," he answered.

"Great," I said. "I'm gonna take a walk for a bit, I'll be back in a little while."

"OK," he grinned, "don't get lost."

Outside in the streets there were sounds, car engines, horns, laughter, music from bars and open windows. I felt a tingle in my flesh coming from the outside and warming its way inward, the holiday party sounds were crawling over and through my flesh. My head in an acid fog, I walked along the streets. Old houses needing paint, littered streets, people walking, holding each other, smiling as they picked their way between the garbage cans that lined the way to the beach.

Once at the beach I heard rougher party sounds. Past a heap of beer cans, I found the party--the bikers, both packs, were having their celebration on the beach. A huge bonfire made them seem to glow in a strange unearthly light. Denim vests patched with emblems, firelight flickering off polished chrome, couples dancing or groping on the sand, plenty of people, plenty of beer.

Ignoring the cycle hounds, I sat on the beach looking to the sea. The sun had just gone down, twilight barely past, and I was beginning to peak on the acid. Leaning my head back I felt my brain soaring, screaming high, racing to meet itself amid the waves. I felt as if I was underwater, my eyes closed. I could sense very little from the outside world, just a muffled roar coming from the party. I flew, swam, skimming over and through the sea. The colors in my head were better than anything outside, so my eyes remained tightly shut. I was above, beyond, far from the party, the beach anything.

Suddenly, coming up to meet me and pull me down came the roar, growing, crawling inside my head. I could hear it growing; I could distinguish screams and shouts. It was so much easier to decide what was happening behind my own eyelids than to open them to a world of nonreality reality.

Though the colors pounded my heavy eyelids, I finally had to open them. The roar became too strong to ignore any longer. When my eyes opened, they flashed in shock at the scene. The beach was in turmoil; the Jokers and Madcaps were pushing, shoving and pummeling each other all over the sand. Swinging his fists like a pair of deadly hammers, one huge biker sent two of his adversaries sprawling in a bloody heap on the beach.

Looking at the downed, wounded figures, I suddenly became afraid. I didn't know what started it; I didn't care. Frightened, I ran, ran away from the beach, away from the denim-vested brutes as they fought each other on the shore. Colors flashing inside me, images of blood and pain, overcame beauty. In blind terror I ran, like a child from a nightmare. As I fled down a side street, I found myself thrown up against a wall as about twenty more chops went by me, headed for the battle. I didn't see what patch they were flying, but they were shouting curses and several had heavy chains draped around their necks.

I pressed myself against the wall, afraid of the blood, afraid of the nightmare violence. Someone else's blood, someone else's violence. Fear, like a black fog, came over me as I pressed against the wall. I slowly loosened my grip on the unreal corner of nothing and sank to my knees. I began to laugh, lightly, to myself, then heartily out loud for all to hear. By god, I realized the whole scene wasn't real. It was all inside me. I couldn't die; I couldn't be hurt, not by them. I had no reason to fear. I laughed. I heard more shouting from the beach and the wail of police sirens, and I laughed.

I discovered immortality in my drugged mind. I would float above everything. Nothing could hurt me because I was not a part of anything, pain, violence, nothing. Let them fight their battles, win or lose their wars. It wasn't a part of me. I could leave it all to them.

Calmed by the realization of my own power, I made my way back to Eric and the band. The sun had gone down; my trip had peaked, and I was coming down. When landing from an acid journey, I always want to return, and at the same time wonder where I had been. In a fog, I found myself returning to the people I'd met on my way up.

We went to work loading the truck with equipment for the night's performance. The band was second on the bill, so we had a few hours to make it there and set up. The feeling was happy, careless. No one seemed concerned about anything as we went about our business.

"Here, Ken," said the bass player, Peter Music.

"Huh? Oh yeah, thanks man," I said accepting the offered number.

"Hungry?" asked Peter. "Eric's gone off for food. No telling what he'll bring back, no meat though."

I took a hit from the number and passed it back. "Yeah, I'm hungry. Maybe its just the munchies, but I could sure do with some food."

"Did I hear someone say food?" It was Eric back already. "I was so spaced out I hadn't noticed him coming or going."

"O.K. man," laughed Peter. "What did you bring back, a McDonald's hamburger?"

"Perish the thought!" cried Eric, throwing his arm across his eyes in a dramatic gesture. "Some poor beast laid down his life for those burgers. I respect the sacred cow...however, I've never heard of sacred crabs and four bottles of wine.

In no time at all we were off, driving down the road, eating crab and drinking wine. I was still tripping, the rushes were still spinning my mind into unexplored space, but the wild insane fear on the beach was gone. I was mellowing out smoothly, and I was coming down in a fine glide.

"Ken?" Peter asked, "where did you come from before here?"

"Well, until yesterday, I was living in a hollow log in Big Sur," I said. "I left this morning, cleaned up in Carmel, hustled a couple of bucks, went to the road and Eric picked me up."

"That's far out," he said, "but what I meant was, why are you just traveling and living on the streets? I'm not knocking it, ya know. I'm just being curious."

I looked at him, took a long pull on the wine and said, "Yeah, well I really don't know." I handed him the wine, and he smiled a warm sort of understanding smile.

The gig was to be at a small coffee house called the Tiki Room. The Polynesian atmosphere was supposed to attract exotic people, but like most of the small clubs, all it did was attract freaks who wanted a place to rap on each other and listen to nice sounds. The band liked the place, liked the audience, and, in turn, was always well received.

For about fifteen minutes, I wheeled amps on stage, set up lights, put extra drum sticks by the drums, and did a few more odds and ends. When I finished, I sat down at the table with Eric, who paid me and ordered a glass of juice for me.

No alcohol was sold in the Tiki Room, so I settled back with a glass of pineapple juice. I took a long drink of the sour sweet drink and smiled. So far that day I had ingested, LSD, hashish, marijuana, beer and wine. In comparison, the juice seemed so peaceful that I completely lost what was left of the shaking fear I had found on the beach.

I was relaxing, enjoying the last mild rushes of the acid as I listened to the band, when Eric spoke up.

"Ken, this is Nancy and Carole."

"Huh!" I started, I had been so deep in my own thoughts that I hadn't noticed that two girls had joined us. "Hi there," I said, "sorry for not paying attention."

"It's O.K.," said Nancy with a laugh. "How do you know Eric," she asked, pulling her chair closer to him.

"Oh, he found me on the road by Carmel and put me on to a little coin," I said.

"What were you doing in Carmel?" asked Carole, as Nancy and Eric became lost in their own conversation.

"Just passing through, that's all," I said with a smile.

She answered with a grin and a wink and soon we were engaged in our conversation about highways and California sunshine. "Here, Kenny, try this," she said holding out her hand.

"Thanks, what is it?" I asked, taking the white capsule from her outstretched palm. She brightened up, her small round face dominated by a large smile of pride.

"It's real organic mesc. I'm not kidding. I just did one myself." With a slight chuckle, I dropped the cap and washed it down with the last of my harmless pineapple juice.

"Hey man," Eric said. "The band's going to leave their gear here at the club tonight 'cause they've got an afternoon set tomorrow. So we're done for now. Nancy wants to know if we want to see a flick at the drive-in outside town. They've got a van!"

"Great, why not?" asked Carole, grabbing my arm, her eyes sparkling, her long dark hair falling in dirty curls to her shoulders. "We could trip to a movie."

"Well, far out!" I laughed, and we left the club. Eric and Nancy ran back to his car for the last of the wine as Carole and I made our way to the van. She had a lot of energy bottled up inside her as she ran ahead of me. I felt a little tired and didn't even try to keep up. She turned and rammed her hands into the back pockets of her jeans, calling for me to hurry. Her bare feet hopped up and down on the pavement, making her small breasts jiggle in her halter top.

"Come on, Kenny, hurry it up," she laughed. "We can have the back, I don't want to drive."

I didn't want to drive either, so I hurried and we rolled

into the back as Eric and Nancy came running down the
street. Eric was elected to drive, with Nancy sitting beside
him giving directions. Carole and I took possession of the
mattress in the back. I reached into my pocket, got my stash,
and as we drove around Palo Alto, I rolled a few numbers,
handing some up front.

In a slow, easy, rising way I was beginning to feel the
mesc. Looking around to where Carole was sitting I smiled to
her and to myself. "Not bad, is it man?" she said, returning
my smile. "I'm getting off in a fine mellow way."

"Thanks lady, me too," I said as I felt myself rising with
a slow movement, "My hands seemed to belong to a slow
motion film as I passed a joint to Carole while Eric guided the
van into the drive-in.

"Hey, who paid, man?" I called up front to Eric as he
adjusted a speaker in the window.

"No hassles, man," laughed Nancy, "I know the chick at
the gate. Didn't you hear me talk to her?"

"Uh no, I guess I didn't," I muttered in a confused way.

"Wow, you two must be getting off fine," said Eric with a
quick grin.

"You'd better believe it, man," said Carole from behind
me as she put her arms around my neck and planted a kiss on
top of my head.

I looked up to the screen where Jane Fonda was seducing
some detective named Klute. "Man," I muttered, "What is
this flick all about?"

"Eric," I heard Nancy say, "Screw this movie. Let's go
explore."

"Great," he answered, "We can go look at people."

"Look at people? What do you mean look at people?" I
asked, having no idea what they were talking about.

"Just that, dude," he laughed, "go look at 'em."

"You mean somebody just sitting in his car is going to
turn around and find you staring at him?"

"Yup," Eric answered as he and Nancy hopped out of the
van. I began to laugh as I imagined what a citizen of Amerika
would feel like when confronted with Eric's thin hair-covered
face peering at him through a car window. It was ridiculous
but funny in an absurd way, and I laughed harder and fell
back on the mattress. It was a wild, unreal holiday. I wasn't
sure where I was, who I was with. Her name was Carole. She

gave me mescaline.

Carole moved over to me, and I put my head in her lap as we watched the end of the first movie. With her hands stroking my hair, I let my mind go for a moment. Soaring high, leaving the sensations of my body for a moment, I floated high amid the darkened clouds of a California night. Feeling the mellow rushes of her fine dope and the tender touch of her hands on my forehead, I settled back, eyes closed and enjoyed the stoned female company I had missed over the last few weeks.

"Oh, wow!" I exclaimed as I opened my eyes, shaken from my lofty flight by the theatre's display of their Independence Day fireworks. Clutching Carole's hand, I gaped at the show. Explosions, colors and lights, inside, outside, lighting up my eyes from both directions. It was a holiday. I was in Palo Alto with Carole, tripping on mescaline. I half rose from her lap and felt myself joining the rockets, my eyes glowing, living embers inside my head, bursting with the rockets.

As the bombs exploded, Carole rolled next to me on the mattress. Fireworks, her warm, winding, moist body grasping and arching beneath me. The flashes of exploding color splashed on her sweating forehead and closed eyes. We moved into each other as the colorful display of reds, greens, blinding whites and yellows splayed over our naked bodies. Her thighs, warm and holding, flashed from livid red to warm pink, her breasts, small and firm to my wandering fingers, seemed alive with moving living, changing colors. Holding, gasping, wanting each other. This night we mixed our passions. It was a holiday trip, and we didn't want to come down.

The fireworks ended in a panoramic display of lights as her hands clutched my hair and her heels dug into the back of my thighs. And a moment later, all was done. Our sweaty tired bodies fell beside each other on the mattress. I turned and lightly kissed her eyes. She smiled and stroked my forehead with her soft hand and whispered something I couldn't hear.

We lay there together and slowly wound down. We watched the last movie, neither of us knowing what it was. We just lay there relaxed, the chill of the evening cooling our sweaty forms. Holiday or not, we had to come down.

The movies ended. Eric and Nancy returned. We didn't know where they'd been and we didn't ask. We all headed back for the Tiki Room and Eric's car.

"Kenny," said Carole as we stood beside the van saying our goodbyes outside the Tiki Room. "Where are you going from here?"

"I really don't know," I said, "Up to San Francisco for a bit, maybe lay around Telegraph in Berkely." My hands were jammed inside my jacket pockets. I shrugged my shoulders and continued, "I didn't plan to be here. Two months ago a chick and I were on the East Coast talking about Oakland and heading for Iowa. So wherever the good rides go, I guess."

I looked down at my scuffed, worn boots. I almost felt like asking her if I should stay, asking her if she would like me to stay or want me to stay. I looked up to find her looking down at her bare feet on the pavement.

"Yeah, well," she said slowly, "I can dig that; I just want you to have a good life, you know?"

I couldn't say anything more. I didn't even know her last name and she didn't know mine. I couldn't ask someone who was a part of a holiday mescaline trip to become part of tomorrow and let tonight become yesterday. I couldn't ask her and she didn't ask me, so I stood there for another minute, then said, "Yeah, you too. Take care."

"Hey, Ken, come on!" Eric called from the door of the Tiki Room. He had just opened it with a key I didn't know he had, and was waiting for me to help him check the gear.

"Looks good," he said after a quick inventory. "Let's go find my car and crash out. I'm really wasted."

After a day of heavy tripping, of leaving people I had lived with, known and loved that morning, and finding, knowing and leaving someone else that night, I too felt wasted. "Yeah man," I sighed, "good idea."

I was tired, very tired. I just wanted to curl up in my bedroll for a long night's sleep. Slowly, silently we walked along the street, feeling a slight breeze blowing on our faces. The pavement seemed cold and hostile to my feet, wearing the heels and souls of my boots down and into nothing.

I thought of how far I had come this day, this Independence Day holiday. The road from Big Sur to Palo Alto must be at least a million miles long. My mind, a jumble of thoughts and confused emotions, needed rest, no cares or worries, just sleep. My old battered bedroll seemed almost like a refuge.

"Hey man, its gone!" Eric exclaimed.

"What's gone, man," I muttered, still lost in my own thoughts.

"My car, my car's been ripped off!" he said and ran over to the curb where he had left it.

"What, good lord!" I exclaimed, shaken back to my senses by the loss. "Could anyone have borrowed it?"

"It's possible." he answered, "Look, I'll call the cops and see if they know anything, then start checking out a few people."

In a few minutes a patrol car came, and Eric gave the men inside a description of the car. I stood back a bit, police generally made me nervous and I was still half stoned and in no shape to talk to them, even if it was a legitimate reason. Eric waved for me to come over and reluctantly I did. "Yeah, what's up?" I asked.

"Look, they want one of us to go with them to drive the car back if they find it, so you go, OK? I'm going to check out those people."

I had been given a lot of rides over the years, but at four in the morning, coming down from acid, dope, wine and mescaline, a ride in the back seat of a Palo Alto patrol car just didn't seem normal.

I sat there as we drove along, about nodding out from exhaustion. My mind was slowly wandering. I thought of the car, about why there wasn't a wire mesh screen between the seats. Unconsciously I patted my pocket and suddenly remembered the dope.

"Jesus," I muttered, "I hope I look straight."

"What's that, son?" asked one of the men in uniform.

"Oh nothing, sir, just thinking out loud!" I said brightly.

Just then our brief conversation was cut short by their radio. "It's all right, son; they've found the car," said the policeman. "Someone borrowed it while you guys were gone. Your friend says it's all right, just a good friend needing a car."

"That's great," I said, feeling almost awake. I'll get to leave these guys, I thought; imagine being with cops and not being busted.

They let me out by a house just two blocks from where Eric had first parked the car. "Uh, like thanks for the ride, guys," I said as I crawled out of the car. "Have a nice whatever."

"Hello there, junior patrolman," laughed Eric. "One of the guys in the band drove it home for me!"

"Great man, just great," I laughed, shaking my head, "Like that's a little heavy man, a weird ride."

"I'm sorry, man," said Eric in an almost serious voice. "I bet that was a bit much. Here's where we flake out anyway, and if you're as tired as you look, you'll sleep forever."

"Thanks, man, god knows I'm wasted," I said. "If ya don't mind, I'll flop here in the front yard." I wanted to sleep outside because the cool night air did more good than anything else in helping me sleep.

"Anywhere you want. Good night," said Eric with a quick grin and wink as he skipped inside.

Slowly I unrolled my bedroll, feeling with the ease of long association, every bump and fold in its fiber. I crawled inside, easing my tired body into the warmth of its fabric. My head rested on my pack, my hair in tossled waves fell over the flag sewn on top. I turned my head and settled down to sleep. My mind was fogged. Where was yesterday? I had come so far today and had a long way to go tomorrow. Slowly, coming down a long slide, I drifted into sleep.

The sun was high when I woke. I crawled out of the damp bedroll, shaking my head to clear its grogginess. I looked up to the sky and saw how late it was. My bedroll was still a bit wet from the morning dew, but the morning was long gone. I turned my head and saw Eric sitting on top of his car, having a private conversation with a bird in a nearby tree.

For a moment I didn't remember him; he was part of a very foggy yesterday that seemed long ago. The morning, the day, however, felt real and I knew it was time to leave, time to look at a highway alone.

"Ken," Eric said as I prepared to leave, "we still need a roadie. Like I said, it don't pay much, but it's more than you're making now."

"Thanks, Eric. But it's really time for me to leave."

"You're sure?"

"Yeah, man. Thanks anyway."

"O.K. then. Have a happy."

"For sure, fella--bye."

I caught a ride to north 101 and sat there on the ramp, waiting for a ride. I was thinking of San Francisco, Oakland, and the miles ahead of me, miles which I didn't know where they would take me, and I heard the roar of bikers again. This time on the highway, hair flowing wild, riding hard came a large pack of outlaws. I chuckled a bit when I saw their patches. Gypsy Jokers and Madcaps riding together as friends.

I wondered what had happened to their holiday war. Yesterday must have become long ago for them too.

Shaking my head, I looked for the next car and put my thumb out.

WINDOWS

There were a few lights breaking through the darkness, from taverns, apartments and street lights, but for the most part the streets of the city were dark. It was two or three in the morning in Salt Lake City as I slowly walked along the streets. I watched the houses and the buildings. I thought of this city, of Brigham Young leading his people across the mountains, arguing and quarreling with their guide, Jim Bridger, the first man to ever see the Salt Lake and the greatest mountain man of them all.

I thought of the history of this town, the crop-saving sea gulls, the monument of temple square and a religion I knew so little about. As I looked toward the temple, I could see the moon peering at me between the gothic roofs of the buildings.

I wasn't sure when or why I had decided to come here. After leaving Palo Alto, I just spent some time in San Francisco, Oakland and Berkely. In Berkely I had laid some flowers by the fence at the deserted site of People's Park. The flowers were in memory of James Recter, killed during the battle for the park about two years earlier.

After Berkely, I camped on the beach at Mendicino and drifted to a few communes in the area. And somehow, thirty six hours ago, I found myself in Reno, Nevada, and decided to keep going east for a while.

Utah had always been hostile to me. Over the years, I had been hassled in Cedar City, Spanish Fork, Ogden and Provo. For some reason though, Salt Lake City had always been friendly, and as usual when I walked down its streets, I felt a warm happiness at being here.

The few lights that shone in the night weren't grabbing and clutching me like the neon wonders of Vegas or Reno. They softly laid colored patterns on the sidewalks at my feet; they were soft, easy lights.

I stopped at an all-night coffee shop. My packs were feeling a bit heavy, and I was glad to throw them into a corner and rest myself at the counter. The waiter, a kid of about seventeen, left off reading his paper to serve me.

"Hot tea, please," I said, looking at the empty cafe.

Curiously, he asked, "Are you hungry?"

"A little," I said, "but a little short too."

He looked at me. I had thrown my leather jacket on the floor atop my packs, displaying my dust-encrusted travel clothes. His eyes went to my filthy open-necked blue denim shirt and the beads around my neck, then to the counter where my hands rested with their dirty, bitten fingernails. Finally, his eyes rested on my wrist and a bracelet I was wearing. A couple of years earlier, I had needed a place to crash in Jackson Hole, Wyoming. An old Indian woman had given the porch of her souvenir shop. We had talked far into the night, and in the morning when it was time for me to go, she had given me a bracelet to remember her by. It was a 1921 silver dollar on a silver bracelet, and I had worn it in her memory every since.

"Hey, I like that," the waiter said, pointing to the bracelet.

"Thanks," I answered, raising my arm for him to see it better, "I've had it for a long time."

"Can I give you twenty-five dollars for it."

"No," I said, "I wouldn't sell it. Sentimental value, you know? Thanks anyway."

"Fine. Look, man, have a hamburger too, on me. I can see you're hungry."

"Well, thank you. Thanks a lot," I said, smiling at him, and it was a smile that included the whole city this night.

I left the cafe and wandered through the better part of the city. I found a fine, stately-looking house with a large yard and several trees and bushes in the rear and went to sleep. The town always seemed peaceful, maybe because I always arrived completely wasted and was able to sleep.

The next morning, I wandered through the city. Sitting on the sidewalk of the downtown area, I watched a pan-handling freak blow a trumpet to attract passers by. The midmorning shoppers were coming in and going out of shops, some smiling at me, some ignoring me, everyone just going about their business. A dog came by and sniffed at my pack, licked my hand when I petted it, and left. Watching the dog trot down the street, I shook my head and softly smiled inside.

I got my packs together and started walking. That

tranquil, pleasant morning would only exist for a brief time. I knew if I stayed, that feeling would be gone, broken, as the day grew longer. If I left now with this morning, this moment swelling inside me, its memory would stay with me for a long time.

Looking back up the hill, I saw the temple, the figure of an angel blowing a trumpet shone above the town like a herald calling farewell. I headed for a northern highway. That way was Montana, mountains, maybe the cool shade of a tree, work in the copper mines of Butte or a look at the college at Missoula. I didn't know exactly what I was headed for.

By noon I was on my way north, well away from Salt Lake, uncomfortable in the hot midday sun. The towns were far apart and the rides were a long time coming. I felt dirty. I hoped that I would find a place to take a bath soon. I hadn't had a full bath in a week. That morning I'd cleaned up in a gas station, but that kind of cleaning doesn't stay long. I had changed my shirt, the dirty denim to a grey cotton with a red scarf to protect my neck. The jeans were filthy, torn, faded and patched; a once colorful flower design trimmed the legs, but now dust covered the pattern. I sat looking at my packs, thinking of the times when they were new. I remembered when I had painted "Trans-Amerika" on the front of the pack and sewed the flag on the top, "Trans-Amerika" written in the white stripes. It felt so long ago. My thumb rose as a car passed, then stopped a little ahead.

By nightfall I was in a town somewhere in Idaho, tired and sleepy once more. The town was kind of pretty, a small town, but clean and hopefully having a place to rest. It was dark, and I was sleepy, so I really didn't see too much that night. Most of the lights were off--a quiet town that turned itself in after nightfall. I didn't crave any kind of excitement, just rest. A sign said there was a park about eight blocks away, so I slowly trudged on up the street.

The night was a bit cold, colder than last night. The altitude must have changed. My leather jacket warmed me some, but my legs, covered only by worn denim, were cold. I was tired, not just the tired of needing sleep, but an inside tired, a weariness of the kind of life I was living. On nights like this, I would think; I had to think. When I was riding in a car with the engine pulling me along a road I could lie back, look at the world flashing by me at 60 miles an hour and get stoned on that feeling. If I planned to travel all day and all night, I would light a number or drop a tab or cap and be stoned on that. Tonight, though, I was completely straight and needed sleep. Until I slept, however, I would have to put up with my mind.

I was tired, tired of feeling dirty, tired of being afraid of the police, tired of being sleepy with no place to go, and most of all I was tired of being alone. I was a thumber, someone alone on a highway that another person picks up and travels with for awhile. No matter how close I felt to anyone I met, I knew at sometime their highway would go north and mine south. At times, most times, it was actually easier that way. It took no real effort to feel love for one day or one night. The most burning, intense love imaginable was no problem for me--for one day or one night. The love for a woman, the friendship of a man. It was easy to wave goodbye, shoulder my packs and cross the freeway, remembering them, missing them. It was so simple to feel for a moment, a time, but to sustain those feelings, to work at love, to reach into the innermost depths of myself and offer myself completely was not so simple and uncomplicated, so I left. Perhaps I preferred short, beautiful memories to the long, difficult relationships. Perhaps that is why I was alone.

"Sure I can love. I know I can; I have before. I will again," I said to myself as I fingered the beads around my neck. The beads had been given to me a year earlier. I loved her; I loved her husband and their child. I had been with them two days. I remembered the bracelet the kid wanted to buy. I loved the woman who had given it to me. I had been with her one day. I remembered holding a girl all night, looking at the stars or the fog on a creek in the early morning. I had felt love for her as we touched and I looked into her eyes. I stayed with her a month. I always left though, and the people just became memories as I waited by a hundred road sides to fall in love again.

In this town tonight, I was forced to think since I was too tired to tune myself out. I walked along the street heading for the park and the rest I needed.

"Hey, son of a bitch!"

Someone screamed and I heard the crash of a bottle at my feet.

I turned to see a car pull up about half a block from me and four grease pile out.

"Ya fucker, you come'er! Move bastard!"

All I could think of was, "Oh no! Oh my god, no! I'm not ready!"

I was afraid, scared of their looks, T-shirts on a cold night like this. Jeans, heavy boots, thick black belts, scowls, sneers and short combed hair. One still had a bottle of beer in his hand as he debated whether to finish it or throw it.

It crashed at my feet when he threw it. "Like it, fucker?" he yelled as I jumped back.

I couldn't say anything; I was much too afraid. If I tried to speak, I would just stammer and frighten myself all the more. None of them were bigger than I, so I decided to try to back them off. If I could hurt one of them, maybe the rest would back off.

I threw my packs on the sidewalk and jumped backwards toward a closed gas station, all the time my silent voice screaming for help. If someone noticed what was happening, maybe I would get help. I pulled my knife and started backing toward the station.

"You gonna' use it, prick?"

"All right, mother, you're gonna' die!"

I kept backing, hoping when they closed, I could cut just one of them.

At that moment, I heard a police siren and a cry of "Hold it!" I saw the flashing lights and black and white patrol car. I was relieved. My legs felt as if they would give out under me. The grease stood there, looking at each other and at the two policemen moving toward them.

I sheathed my knife and waited to be asked if I wanted to press charges when they arrested the hoods. I wasn't tired anymore. Their park wasn't a resting place for me. I walked back to my packs on the sidewalk between the patrol car and myself. I would be glad to travel all night just so I could leave this town.

"All right, come over to the car."

Was he talking to me? One policeman was talking to the grease, but hadn't put them in the car yet.

"Now, kid."

"Huh?" The other one pushed me over to the car and made me put my hands on the hood, spreading my legs so he could pat me down. I looked over my shoulder and saw the cop who was talking to my attackers, patting them on the shoulder and sending them off. Smiling and shaking his head, the cop walked toward the car. He was tall and thin and had kind of a worn face that looked sad even if he was happy.

"All right, Sam, what's this one got?" he said, sounding as if I was just a nuisance rather than someone who'd just been attacked in his town.

"Just this," said the cop who searched me, "here." He handed the other policeman my knife.

"Fine. O.K., kid, into the back," he said as he took my knife and gave me a slight shove. The other cop retrieved my gear. He held up my pack as he strode back toward the car. He was younger than the first cop and a lot bigger--no taller, but he weighed at least 200 pounds without any of that in fat. Pointing to the flag on the pack, he laughed and said, "Look, Gary, this one's a goddamned patriot!"

"What a town. I'm not ready for this, Christ, I just wanted to crash out here," I thought as I rode in the back of the car. Sam and Gary were up front, not looking at me nor trying to start any sort of conversation. I managed to eat the two numbers I had left without them noticing. I felt relieved about that when suddenly I remembered that I still had one hit of mescaline in my pack and no way to get at it without their knowing.

They hustled me into the station to an old, weary desk sergeant who looked like he really needed to be home in bed. They threw my packs into the corner across the room from me, the mesc still inside.

"All right, put the contents of your pockets on the desk."

"Take off your clothes."

"Bend over."

Ouch! Damn that hurt! What the hell did they think I had up there, a shotgun?

They gave me back my clothes and threw me into a cell with about ten other prisoners. Most of the men were asleep except one other freak on leave from the Navy who'd been busted for robbing a drug store. We talked for awhile then crashed out.

I looked up to the ceiling and bright light enclosed by wire mesh about twelve feet above me, and smiled to myself, thinking that I was finally going to get some sleep. It wasn't where or how I'd planned, but I could finally sleep, and I'd better get used to it because I would probably be here for quite a while.

I thought of what they might charge me with. They didn't bust the grease for anything, and I had a knife, so I might be nailed for assault with a deadly weapon. When they found the chemical in my pack, they would nail me for that as well. I looked up to the light again, deciding it would be my companion for a spell. I said good night to the light, rolled over and went to sleep.

Morning, early morning. I was tired when they hustled me out of the cell and to the day court. What was I charged with? Did they find the mesc? It was early--would they feed me?

"Hitchhiking within the city limits, ten dollar fine, three dollars court costs, pay the bailiff."

"What?" I thought to myself. "Where's the grease? What about the knife? I'm not guilty! What about the drugs in my pack?" I wasn't thinking too clearly, but luckily, I didn't say anything except, "Guilty, sir. I'll pay and leave."

I had fifteen dollars when I'd come to this town; by Trans-Amerikan standards, I was fairly well off. And now I had only two dollars left.

Another sergeant was at the desk when I went to get my stuff back.

"Here, Kid," he said. "Your knife, wallet, packs. Is that all?"

"Yessir."

"We'll give you a lift out of town...and don't come back."

"Yessir," I said again. "I won't." I looked at my packs. They hadn't been searched. I didn't know why, but I was very thankful. With only two dollars left, I figured I'd better head north and seriously try to find work in the copper mines of Butte, Montana.

A silent policeman drove me to the edge of town. "What a night," I thought as we rode along. "What a town." I had slept well in their jail and had been lucky in their court, so I might as well be thankful for that at least. The car stopped by the interstate on ramp. I got out, threw my gear on my shoulder and started walking. I turned to look back at the police car, perhaps to wave, but he was gone, back to town.

CHRISTIAN COMES TO VANITY FAIR

I looked out the window at the Idaho landscape, high hills, distant mountains, a few trees and fewer buildings. I didn't know how far it was to the Montana border, but I figured I was pretty close and would be in Butte by mid-afternoon.

It felt strange to be awake and traveling today. Maybe last night never existed or maybe I was still in jail, dreaming of today. I smiled to myself as I looked across the seat at the driver of the car. A man, like a thousand other men, friendly, curious and generous enough to give me a ride as far as he could. A man I would never get to know very well because very soon I would leave his car and continue on my way and he on his, both ways separate. "Today is real, all right," I thought as I turned once more to the window and landscape that stretched forever.

The driver turned off the interstate after twenty minutes or so, apologizing for not being able to take me further and accepting my hand in a brief but real show of friendship.

I walked along the highway for a bit until I came to the merging point of the next on ramp, threw my packs on the pavement and sat down. The sun was slowly climbing through the sky and the day was getting hotter. I took the scarf from my neck and wiped my sweating face, looking down the road for more cars, chances for rides. I replaced the scarf as a truck stopped on the off ramp where my last ride had let me off. I reached into my pack for my canteen when I saw why the truck had stopped, another thumber got out of the truck and headed toward me. I watched and saw that the thumber was a girl carrying a large suitcase.

"Well, she ain't no freak," I thought, "I wonder where she's going."

She walked toward me, lugging her suitcase which seemed much too heavy for any sort of walking travel. She waved with her free hand, and I waved back. As she got closer, I saw that she was tall--a bit taller than I anyway--with short curly red hair and a flowered pant suit.

"She sure hasn't been on the road long," I thought. "Must be just going to the next town." I smiled to myself. There is really a kind of snobbery that Trans-Amerikan freaks have toward casual hitchhikers.

"Hello," I said when she got close enough to hear. "Want a drink? It's warm, but wet."

"Oh, thanks," she said with an accent nearly British, but not British at the same time, more Canadian or Australian. "Where are you going?"

"That way," I said, pointing north.

"Really?" she said. "So am I. I'm going to Canada. Alberta. Where 'that way' are you going?" she asked, also pointing north.

"Well, no place really, I guess. Why?"

"You won't believe this, but I was traveling with two guys who were supposed to take me back there, but last night they decided to try to find work in Pocatello. So I'm going back by myself...and I'm afraid."

"Why didn't you take a bus back?" I asked, knowing that she did have cause to worry.

"I don't have any money. Those guys were paying for everything and when I wouldn't stay with them for the rest of the summer, they got pissed and wouldn't give me anything to get back on." She looked lost and forlorn as she said it, hints of tears in her eyes as her lower lip trembled slightly.

"I'm sorry," I said, "but I'm pretty well broke, too; otherwise I'd put you on a bus myself. With that gear," I said, pointing to her suitcase, "you're really not set for thumbing."

"I know it. I'm not used to hitchhiking. I've never done it before. Will you come with me?" she asked, her eyes pleading.

I had a lot of questions about what she was doing traveling with two guys who would just dump her in the middle of Idaho, or why she would trust me when we'd just met. Then again, when did I get to be any sort of moralist?

"Well, why aren't you afraid of me? You don't know me at all," I said, voicing at least one of my questions.

"I don't know. Maybe because you gave me a drink," she said with the beginnings of a happy gleam in her eyes.

"Actually, I'm very dangerous," I said grinning at her.

"Oh, you!" and she slapped my arm, starting us both laughing as if we were a couple of kids with a dirty book.

"O.K., O.K.," I said, trying to catch my breath, "I'll take you to Canada. How do we get where you want to go? By the way, if it makes any difference, I'm Kenny."

"And I'm Debbie, and we just stay on this road all the way across the border."

A car with a trailer pulled over after we'd been together for about an hour. She ran over to it to find out where they were going, and I just sat back and waited. I rarely asked anyone how far they were going, especially in the middle of the Great Amerikan West, when many hours are spent waiting for a ride. However, couples find it much easier to catch rides. Maybe they seem harmless or helpless or something. Whatever the reason, a guy with a chick can afford luxuries, like asking how far a potential ride is going.

"Hey, Kenny, come on! They're going to Canada!"

"Well, far out," I said, picking up our gear and taking off running.

The car was filled with boxes and packages as if a major move was taking place. Crowded together, we jammed ourselves, her suitcase and my packs, into the back seat.

A small, handsome, well-dressed man was driving while a cowboy rode next to him. Next to the cowboy was a mousey-looking woman who just seemed to be there.

They told us they were going to Montreal to build a shopping center. The driver's father owned a construction company, and Junior was going to manage this particular job. The cowboy, named Joe, had been hired the day before to run a machine. Junior and Joe met in a bar and after a few beers and a few drinks, Joe had been hired at an outrageous salary and asked to go to Montreal.

I sat back and relaxed, barely listening to the conversations, just letting the engine pull me along the highway. Rides like this seldom interested me. I don't know why. The people were people just the same as were the residents of Trans-Amerika, but there was a culture gap of some sort. Their interests weren't the same as mine; their view on life, politics, drugs, anything at all were simply not the same as mine and rather than argue, I generally kept silent. I appreciated the ride of course, but I could only thank them in virtually hollow words and save my feelings for someone else.

As I sat there, I began to catch pieces of the conversation in spite of myself.

"Did you guys have to drink so damned much?" the woman was asking. "Fuck, you just met each other!"

"Yeah, as a matter of fact we did. We had a good time, bitch, so shut up or I'll leave you here in Montana," Junior retorted.

Joe wasn't saying anything; he just sat there more or less like me, trying not to pay attention. I was a little afraid of Joe. Cowboys seldom liked freaks, and I had been left with a few bumps to remember them by. But Joe didn't seem at all hostile; he just sat there and looked at the scenery. Maybe he was part of Trans-Amerika, and I couldn't tell. We didn't speak to each other. We weren't driving or controlling anything. We were just being pulled along the highway by someone else's engine.

"But, Jesus, last night was our wedding night!" the woman said, leaning across Joe to look at the driver.

"So what?" her husband answered. "Married or not, you're still a whore, and I'll do what I want."

The woman turned around in her seat to look at us. She was blushing, embarrassed by what her new husband had just said. She seemed relieved to see that Debbie had fallen asleep. The woman had a very pleasant face, not really beautiful, but friendly, a little plump with brown eyes that had a warm, soft shine. Her nose was small, not too small, but small enough to blend in with the rest of her face and not be at all conspicuous. Her mouth broke with a smile that matched her eyes--a friendly, warm smile that brightened her whole face, making the blush seem very becoming, like a royal glow.

"Ken, Debbie says that you're taking her to Canada, and that she met you and asked you to an hour ago."

"Yes, I am, she did," I stammered, beginning to feel stupid, like I had been the victim of some sort of hoax.

"That's really nice of you. What were you doing before that?" she asked, resting both arms on the back of the seat, turning around almost completely to look at me.

I suddenly felt stupid, I don't know why, but I felt like an idiot. I wanted to tell her I was on leave from the Army, going to visit a sick someone someplace, anything that would sound respectable. Maybe it was her eyes or her smile, something about her made me want to appear to be more than a bum. I didn't want to seem like a worthless person when I felt that, despite his money, her husband was just as worthless as any penniless hobo.

In answer to her question, all I could stammer out was, "Nothing much, kind of moving around."

She shook her head and smiled, then asked, "How old are you, Ken?"

"I'm 19, ma'am--why?"

"Call me Cheryl, please; I was just wondering. You seem younger."

"Well, I've had a sheltered life."

At that, she broke into a smile that became a small, light-hearted laugh, and she reached over to rub my greasy hair.

I laughed when she did, and she began to laugh with me. I was glad to see her laugh after the rude put-down her husband had given her.

We began talking, not about anything special, just simple easy conversation. We kept talking and laughing, joking about the weather and looking for humor in the scenery for a long time. We didn't notice when Debbie woke or when the driver turned off the interstate. We continued our merry conversation about nothing until the car stopped.

"All right, everyone, this is Butte," announced Junior. "We're stopping here for awhile. I want to see the town. Anyone in a hurry to get where they're going?"

I looked at Debbie, she shook her head "no" and I said, "No one back here."

He pulled into a motel and parked the car. Debbie looked at me and said, "We'll stay in the car."

"Fuck that shit, you two," said Junior, getting out of the car. "If you're traveling with me, you're traveling first class. Ken, Joe, get the bags. I'll get two rooms."

He came back with two keys and took us into the rooms. He, Cheryl, Debbie and I were to share one room, and Joe had the other. Once inside, we put all the bags in one corner, and I put my packs in another corner.

I looked at Junior and said, "Do you mind if I take a shower? It's been awhile, like a week."

"Feel free, we'll clean up later," he replied.

I took my pack into the bathroom and dug out a clean set of clothes, set them on the chair and climbed into the shower. The hot water felt so good, I could almost feel the dust of a thousand miles chipping and flaking off my body, turning into mud at my feet. Even a day of travel can leave someone crusted over with dirt, and smelling like a highway. Now, under that spray after six days of travel, I felt reborn, new and clean. My hair had been greasy and my body was sticky until that shower, and as I dried myself off, I thought of how long it would be until the next one.

When I went back to the room with the rest of the travelers, Debbie got up, saying she was next. Junior called me over to join a conversation he and Joe were having about women.

"Do you know how I met Cheryl?" he asked, and without waiting for an answer, continued, "I knew this woman in New Mexico. I used to drink in her place all the time. Dad owned the bar, she just rented it, so she'd give me free drinks. Anyway, I was going to be there for awhile, so I went to this broad and said I needed a fuck for a couple of weeks. She told me that she'd see. Later, she came over to the house I was at and brought Cheryl with her.

"I told Cheryl right away that I would do whatever I wanted, and she better know it. She was there just because I was horny. She understood and didn't complain if I fucked somebody else, so I decided to take her along on this trip. I'm not sure why I married her, but she's got another think coming if she things that makes a difference. I'll still do what I want."

I looked at the guy and decided that I didn't like him at all. On the basis of the story, I guess I shouldn't have liked Cheryl either, but I did. I liked her eyes and her smile.

"Ken," Junior said, "I'll tell you why I picked you two up. I wanted to get laid, and I wonder if that girl in there is willing," he added, pointing to the bathroom. "Do you have any claim on her--or is it like she said, you just met?"

"Yeah," I said, leaning over to him from the chair I was sitting on. "We just met, but if anybody tries anything, and she asks for help, I'll stop'em anyway I can. But I got no claims on her. I hardly know her; she just asked for help and I came along."

"Real good," Junior said. "You know, Ken, guys like you fascinate me. All you want to do is travel around. You never have any money or jobs. How do you live? I mean, if I don't have at least a grand with me, I really feel worried. Shit, I wish I could live like you do. You probably get more bitches than Joe and I ever do, see more things--and all without money. How do you do it, anyway?"

"Yeah, all we want is to travel, nothing else," I thought as I looked at him. "Jesus! You bastard, if you only knew how much people like me want, but they're the kinds of things you haven't even heard of."

"How do you live?" said Junior, interrupting my thoughts.

"Hand to mouth," I replied.

"Yeah, I guess so," he answered and hurried across the room where Cheryl was lying on the bed reading a paperback novel. "Hey, Cheryl! I want to talk to you."

After a few words with her husband, none of which I heard, I only saw her shake her head "no" and then "yes" in response to something he'd said. She went into the bathroom with Debbie when he pointed that way.

Junior returned to me and said, "Cheryl's going to ask Debbie now. Hey, Ken, you'll get that bitch of yours tonight too. I just want to have two tonight--it should be great! You can have Debbie first, then send her to me, and I'll screw 'em both. How's that?"

I had nothing to say at that point. I was in Butte, the place I started for this morning. If Debbie agreed to the arrangement, I'd just leave and head for the mines. If she didn't, we'd both leave and find another ride to Canada.

I had a tendency to fall in love quite often. I had made love to a few women along the way as a result of that tendency--some casually, some not so casually. But in my own way, I had always made love, never just fucked a girl. I didn't try to hit on any available female body whenever I was horny. I wanted the possibility of love. The thought of a premeditated, "Junior-arranged" fuck with Debbie turned me off completely. I started lashing my pack together. If Debbie didn't need my help anymore, I'd be on my way in a minute.

"Ken."

I turned and saw Cheryl coming toward me from the

bathroom. Debbie was behind her but turned to join Junior. I knew she'd agreed, and I prepared to leave.

"Ken?" Cheryl said again.

"Yes, Ma'am," I said, kind of stuttering as I stood up next to my pack.

She looked at my pack, then at the ceiling, then back at me. Her eyes were nervous and her voice was unsteady. "Why do you spell 'Amerika' like that?" she asked, pointing to my pack and its emblem.

I looked at her and grinned. I liked her, I didn't understand why, I just met her. But I really did like her. "Can't spell, I guess," I said. She returned my smile and didn't ask for a better explanation.

"Could we go for a walk? You could show me Butte," she said.

"There's not much to see here. It's a mining town. Lots of slag heaps, that sort of thing, plus everything's kind of dirty and polluted...hey, how'd you know I'd been here before, anyway?" I asked, kind of surprised.

"I didn't," she said. She smiled again, her eyes shining a bit more.

"O.K.," I said. "So let's go look at Butte."

We walked, the woman from New Mexico and the road freak. For a few blocks, we didn't say much. In Butte, there are few sights worth speaking of, so that sort of conversation was ridiculous. Cheryl was the first to break the silence.

"You're planning to leave, aren't you?"

"Yeah, I'm going," I said.

She looked at me and said, "I wish you wouldn't."

"Well, I really don't dig this scene. I think I'd better go."

"Ken," she said, her voice almost trembling, "I heard what my husband told you."

"Yeah," I said, feeling ashamed for both of us--both of us knowing something that was none of our business.

"You think I'm just a slut, don't you?" Her voice raised and her eyes were pleading. "Well, don't you?"

"Look, ah, Cheryl, like it's really not my place to do any judging. I don't even know you," I stammered.

"Yes, but you've heard it, and it's true. We met just like he said. I did ask Debbie to screw him. Now what kind of woman does that?"

She grabbed me, spun me around and looked me in the

eye, almost screaming, "What kind of woman picks up another woman and asks her to fuck for her husband the day after they're married?! What kind of woman does that? For Christ's sake, kid, you're old enough to know better than that, aren't you? You can judge that shit. I'm a slut and a whore!"

"O.K., you are!" I screamed back, "What the hell do you expect me to do about it? I like you. I think you're a nice person. So what if I do? You still think you're a whore, and you'll keep acting like one. I can't help it."

"What kind of man marries a woman just to treat her like a slut? Your old man ain't no great prize, rich father and the whole bit. Hot shit, he still ain't no prize. He ain't no reason for anybody to act like a whore unless she wants it!" I continued.

"Ken, for Christ's sake," and she began to cry, heavy gasping sobs, "I love the fucker. I can't help it, I do. It's not my fault I do."

We were yelling these things at each other in downtown Butte. Passers by stared and walked on. When Cheryl began to cry, she stopped and leaned against a parked car. A man walking by stopped for a moment. I turned and looked at him.

"She's O.K., really," I said and turned back to her. I put my arms around her, and her head rested on my shoulder, dampening my shirt with tears.

"Cheryl, let's go back, O.K.?"

We turned and started back toward the motel.

"Ken," she said looking up from my shoulder where her head still rested, her arm clinging to my waist. "What are you going to do?"

"Well, Debbie agreed, didn't she? I really better go."

"Yeah, she did," Cheryl said, releasing me and straightening up. "I hoped she wouldn't because she loved you. But she did agree."

"Cheryl," I said, "it's now about six o'clock. I met Debbie at about nine or ten this morning. You don't fall in love that quickly."

She turned to me and said, "Don't bet on it."

"O.K., maybe some people do. I haven't, with her anyway, I haven't. I told her I'd get her to Canada safely, but you guys can take care of that. I'll get my gear and split."

"Ken, please don't leave. Stay with us at least for awhile."

"Look," I said, louder than before, "I've got no reason to stay. Believe me, I'd just be in the way."

"No reason!" she screamed, "No reason. Look, I asked you. That's a reason, isn't it? If you stay, maybe Debbie will love you, and my husband will learn to love me!"

"Cheryl, those are a lot of 'maybes' and we both know it won't work out that way," I said to her and softly touched her cheek. "Why kid yourself?"

"I know," she said, taking hold of my hand, "it probably won't work out that way, but please stay. You know, my husband has never seen me cry, but you have."

I smiled and said, "All right. I'll stay for a bit."

We went back to the motel. My gear was where I left it and everyone was watching T.V.

"Where ya' been?" Junior asked lightly.

"Looking at Butte," Cheryl answered. "Ken's been here before."

"Really, Ken?" asked Junior. "Any good bars here?"

"A few," I said, "up the street."

Debbie waved for me to come over to her chair. "Kenny, I'm going to screw you guys tonight, but I'll sleep with you."

"Well, you can sleep with me, of course, but I won't touch you. I'm a celibate."

"A WHAT? You're kidding!"

"Look, I didn't come with you for sex...forget it, I'm just not horny."

"Kenny, you know you're weird, don't you?" she said and laughed.

I stayed four days as Cheryl's friend and Junior's guest.

If the man didn't like the shirt I was wearing or the shoes Debbie had, he would simply buy us replacements. No matter what the subject, whatever the controversy, he would settle it with his wallet. He made no distinctions between objects and people. If he saw something he wanted, he would look for its price tag.

I grew to loathe him and his money. I wanted to break his head open and prove to everyone that the rich are vulnerable too. I wanted to say "no" to the next gift he gave me, or tell him to shut his mouth the next time he insulted someone, anyone. I didn't though. Like a sheep, I followed him, I didn't

know why. Maybe an inherent respect for the man who pays
the bills or a feeling of obligation for the ride and the gifts.
Whatever the reason, I was beginning to dislike myself more
and more. He might not be able to help what he was, but I
could have done something about my involvement with him,
and I was doing nothing.

Everyday I would be determined to leave, and then as the
day went on, change my mind. What changed my mind so
often was Cheryl. In the morning, Junior would take us out
for breakfast, and Cheryl would sit across the table from me
and smile at me. During the day when her husband was
buying gifts for everyone, she would take my hand, and we
would take a walk someplace. Our conversations grew longer
and more serious. She wanted to know about my past, my
family, my travels, my loves.

She would tell me about her family. Her mother and
father were killed when she was twelve, and she had been
raised by her sister and her husband. Her brother-in-law had
seduced her when she was fifteen, and she carried on an
affair with him for almost a year until her sister found out. At
sixteen, she had left school and her sister's house. She'd
been working at odd jobs ever since.

When she couldn't find work, she would, in her words,
"find a man to keep me for awhile." It was in one of those
times that she had met Junior. Some days, she'd seem full of
love and hope for that man and their future together until his
curt tongue and wandering eye would bring her back to
reality. Then she would realize what sort of man he was, and
what sort of marriage she had, and her bright optimism
would turn to dark and lonely despair. Many an hour was
spent with her tear-stained face resting on my chest.

The fourth night in Butte, Junior decided to go to the one
bar in town we hadn't visited. As usual, we all followed
without complaint. We sat at a table in the tavern. It was only
about seven at night and the place was nearly empty. Junior
ordered a round of beer and began a conversation with Joe.

I drank slowly, thinking that in the morning, I had better
leave. No matter what Cheryl said, I knew it would be better
for everyone, myself especially, if I stopped being the guest
of a man I hated.

The cocktail waitress walked by, and I was shaken from
my thoughts by Junior's laugh as he slapped Joe's arm and

said, ''god, I'd like to fuck that bitch. I'll bet she'll put out.''

Joe laughed and said, ''Aren't you getting enough as it is?'' Debbie grinned, and Cheryl glanced at me and lowered her eyes to her glass.

Junior started to smile, ''I want 'em all,'' he said. He signalled the women over and asked for another round. As she left to fill the order, he said again, only louder this time, ''I'll bet she'll put out.''

She returned with the beer looking extremely angry. Junior laid a one hundred dollar bill on the table. ''You want to keep the change?'' he asked. She quickly turned away, but he called her back.

''That?'' he said, and laid another hundred on the table. She began to turn red and angry almost to the point of tears, and silently he laid another hundred on the table. She turned and walked away. She went behind the bar and with shaky hands began to put glasses away.

''Hey, bitch, look!'' Junior yelled and flashed another bill. She ignored him. ''You bitch!'' he yelled and jumped up.

''Easy, man,'' I said, jumping up myself. Cheryl rose too and walked out the door. Junior and I were staring at each other and didn't notice her leave.

''Shut up, kid,'' he said, then turned and walked over to a large man in a grey suit who had just come out of a door to investigate the noise.

''You the owner?'' Junior asked.

''Yeah,'' the man said, raising himself up, looking even larger. ''What's going on here?''

''How much is this place worth?'' Junior asked.

''What the hell...?'' the man gasped.

''I mean,'' said Junior, ''that I want to buy it right now, and I'm serious.''

The man looked over at Joe who sat back in his chair, took a pull on his beer and said, ''He means it--and he can do it.''

''Well, sir, let's go talk,'' the owner said, and took Junior into a back room.

I looked at the woman. I wanted to apologize to her. I wanted to tell her that I thought she was great. I couldn't, though. I was afraid, nervous, the same things that prevented me from decking Junior out prevented me from telling her anything. I figured she would judge me by the company I was keeping, company I had the right to be judged by if I stayed with.

What reason did I have to stay there any longer? This was the fourth day with these people, and I felt ridiculous and ashamed. Sure, I could feel things for Cheryl, but if she was willing to take all the crap from Junior that he gave her, she deserved to be hurt. I couldn't be any sort of alternative for her. At best, I could be her dry towel, and that wasn't any good at all, for either of us.

What was I doing there? I was shaming myself and insulting anyone I met by the company I was keeping.

Junior came out of the room with a smile as big as his face. In his hand was a piece of paper. He approached the woman, who had been standing all this time at the bar, both hands resting on it and looking straight ahead.

"Look, bitch!" Junior's voice filled the room, "I own this place now, see?" and he flashed the paper in front of her. "Get your ass out. You're fired!" Junior watched her as she walked out the back door with his laughter following and hurrying her.

As she left, I looked at Debbie and Joe. They sat at the table joining Junior in his laughter.

It was still early evening, and I figured I might make Billings yet that night. I had no idea why I stayed as long as I had, but the sooner my packs were shouldered and I was trucking down the highway, the better I would feel.

Three nights I had slept with Debbie, not touching her or really wanting to. Three nights I had been drinking with Junior, disgusted by his flashing of bills and writing of checks. Whatever reason I had keeping me here was gone. I was leaving before I grew to hate myself even more. Three nights was more than enough; there wouldn't be a fourth.

I got back to the motel, unlocked the door, threw the key into a corner and went to my packs. They were in a corner by the door, where I'd left them earlier. I ripped off a fancy western shirt that Junior had bought me and put on an old, faded, grey denim work shirt from my pack. I took out my knife and hung it on my belt, tied a scarf around my neck, lashed the packs together and was ready for travel.

"Ken, what are you doing?" It was Cheryl. She was standing in the open doorway, the dark night behind her, making her seem larger than life.

"I'm leaving, Cheryl--goodbye." And I reached into the corner for the key. "Here, your old man might need this," I said, handing it to her.

"Screw that!" she screamed, knocking it to the floor and slamming the door behind her, closing us in the room. "You said you'd stay. Why are you going?" Her voice had changed to a plea.

"Look," I said, "I got no reason to stay. I shouldn't have hung around this long. I don't like your old man. I'm not that nuts about Debbie or Joe either, so I'm leaving before I go crazy being around them."

"Then you don't want to be around me either. It was me who asked you to stay, not them. I don't care about them. I asked you to stay, and if you leave, it's because you don't care about me." Her voice began to break, but she didn't start crying. She walked over to the bed and sat down, her face buried in her hands.

"Look, Cheryl, I didn't say I didn't care for you. I do, very much." I sat down on the bed next to her and put my hand on her cheek to brush away a lone tear that escaped her fingers. "I wouldn't have stayed this long if I didn't care, but you're married to a creep I can't stand, and if I stay, I don't know what will happen."

"O.K., O.K., what about me?" She grasped my hand hard. "What about me? I told you I loved him. Well, I don't know if I do now."

"When I get up in the morning, I look at your bed, at you before I look at him. I walk past your bed as if to go to the bathroom, hoping you'll notice me naked and want me. Last night, I was supposed to be screwing my husband, and I pretended it was you. I tried to see you through the dark while I was holding him."

"You said you didn't have a reason to stay," her voice became soft and she put her hands on my cheeks raising her lips to mine, lightly kissing me. "Let me give you a reason. Let me be your reason."

Our bodies melted together as she pulled me down to her, our lips meeting and grinding together as for a moment we both became a part of each other. Her hand ran itself around my legs and around to my groin. Somehow, I came to my senses and sat up on the bed.

"Ken, honey, what's wrong?" she said as she opened her

eyes.

"What the hell do you think is wrong?" I almost yelled, my voice trembling and shaking. "Sure, you're into a lousy marriage, but I can't help that, only you can. Don't try to make yourself believe that you love me just because I don't like your old man. You don't love me, and I can't love you, and for god's sake, I can't stay with you!"

"How do you know I don't love you?" she screamed back. "What makes you so fucking smart!? How can you tell me what I want or don't want. I've got a brain too, ya' know! I know a few things, and I know what I want." As she said that, she began to cry, not open sobs, but tears filled her eyes and her lip trembled.

I turned to her, grabbed her by the arm and pointed to my packs. "Look, Cheryl. That's me. That's all I have, and that's all I am. Don't kid yourself into loving that. You can't and I can't share it because there's nothing to share with anyone. And nothing for anyone to love."   ·

I left the bed and went to my packs, threw them over my shoulder and opened the door.

Cheryl screamed after me as I walked out the door, "O.K., wise guy! Go on! I don't care, I don't care! If things get a little rough, you can just move on, is that it? Well, then go on. See if I care! Keep it up, and see if anybody cares--ever! Go on, I don't give a damn! I don't care at all!"

Her voice echoed behind me as I half ran to the road. "See if anybody cares--ever!" I wiped my eyes, filled with tears and stinging with pain as I looked back to the motel.

An hour later, I was walking along the Montana section of 194. The night was cold and dark. I hitched up my collar and put my hands in my pockets as I walked. Montana nights are cold. Even in late July.

PART III

FRIENDS, TEARS, ICE AND STRANGERS

"The stillness flowers.
It blossoms and blooms
into something we remembered
yesterday..."

Lyftogt

STILLNESS FLOWERS

My dreams were of trees, tall trees, stretching upward, scraping the clouds and breaking the sunlight into a million flickering light-covered fingers feeling their way to the ground.

The sunlight was replaced by darkness, grey clouds burst open and heavy drops of rain forced their way past the leaves to dampen the earth at the base of the trees.

As the rain fell, my eyes opened slightly. I was a little chilly, and I snuggled deeper into the warmth and darkness of my bed. I remembered many nights in my bed, secure and warm while the storm pounded outside, my blankets warming my naked body. I closed my eyes and was quickly put back to sleep by the steady beat of the rain on my roof.

I slept a while longer and again my eyes opened and again I heard the rain and felt relaxed. I slowly forced myself to wake up, fighting the hypnotic beat of the rain.

As I woke up and my mind cleared, I suddenly sat straight up, throwing water left and right, new drops splashing on my face. I wasn't in bed, and I didn't have a roof, only my leather jacket over my face.

I looked beside me where my boots sat, an inch of rain in the bottom of them, and again to the sky. I laughed to myself and crawled out of my soaked bedroll and emptied my boots. I was already soaked so I wasn't trying to hurry as I put my boots on and threw my gear on my back. The sky was dark with clouds; I couldn't tell the time by the sun. Looking up to the sky and turning to the hill where I was sleeping, I saw a restaurant at the top, just off the road. Packing my soggy gear, I headed to the restaurant, hoping it was open.

"Hey, boy, hurry up!" I looked up, and in the doorway a laughing man was waving at me.

I waved too and began to run, my rain drenched gear weighing me down some. In a minute, I was through the door as the man slapped me on the back.

"Hi, boy," he laughed. He was a large, robust man with an extremely friendly smile, a kind of beardless St. Nicholas. "We don't open for a couple of hours, but the wife and I were watching you down there, wondering when you were going to wake up. When she saw you getting up, she went to make some coffee."

"Well, thank you, sir," I said, holding out my hand. "Thank you, very much. I'm Kenny. I guess I was pretty funny in all that rain."

"You sure were. Here, put that stuff on this counter, boy. Lay 'em over so they'll drip. You can mop it up later."

"Here's coffee. Good morning, son. You look like a drowned rat," said a woman coming out of the kitchen. She was carrying a tray with three steaming cups of coffee. "Sit down, please, both of you. Relax."

We all sat in a circle booth facing the window. I looked out to the dismal morning, dark clouds, heavy rain and a grey sky. I tried to think of where I was. The last city I remembered was Minneapolis, so I figured I was still in Minnesota.

"Hey, come to the earth, boy!" the man said, snapping his fingers under my nose, shaking me back to a damp reality.

"I'm sorry," I said. "Just trying to get my bearings. Where's Minneapolis from here?"

"You from Minneapolis?" The woman asked, leaning towards me a little. She was a nice-looking lady, a duchess in a work print dress and wearing thin glasses.

"No ma'am. I'm coming from Butte. Minneapolis is just the last city I remember before crashing out."

"Well, son, you passed it, about thirty miles west of here. You live in Butte, then?" she continued.

"No, ma'am, I don't. I just spent some time there. It's

just the last place I slept.''

"Well, boy, that's quite a trip. Where are you coming from then?'' asked the man as he put down the coffee cup he had been staring into while his wife and I talked.

"No place, really,'' I said. "Butte and a lot of other places.'' My voice trailed off as I remembered a bar and a motel in Butte, people I would never see again or know what became of their lives. I silently stared ahead, my mind heavy with memories, until the man's voice brought me back to reality.

"Hungry, boy?'' the man asked. "If you haven't slept since Butte, you probably haven't eaten very much either.''

"No, sir, I haven't,'' I said, remembering a few candy bars and donuts given to me the day before.

The woman left the booth and went into the kitchen. "I'll get you a little something for today,'' she said.

"Well then, boy, where the hell are you going? You sure are vague about that,'' the man continued.

I looked at him, his smiling face had grown serious. I wanted to give him an answer. I really did. I couldn't even tell him why I was in Minnesota, because I didn't know myself. I remembered when I left Butte, I was just thinking of leaving town, heading east toward Billings. I didn't stop at Billings, though. I had simply kept going until my exhausted mind and body forced me to sleep. A sleep so deep that I had slept through the better part of a rainstorm and woke east of Minneapolis.

I thought of where I would go from here. Farther east, maybe? I rejected that idea right away and decided to go south, to the town where I'd once lived, where my mother lived, where a lot of friends lived, south of Minneapolis to Iowa.

"Well, sir, I guess I'm going to Iowa!'' I said in an almost bright tone.

"You from Iowa? Where?'' the woman asked as she came back with the three plates of waffles.

I smiled and ladled on the syrup she offered. "I went to high school in Fort Dodge. My mother and quite a few friends live there.''

After breakfast, I cleaned up the mess my dripping gear had made, lashed my packs together and threw them on my back.

"Well, good luck," they said as I walked out the door. The rain had stopped, leaving grey skies and a morning mist. "And try to stay dry, boy!"

I waved and headed for the nearest southbound highway.

* * * * *

"Fort Dodge," I thought. I knew the town well. I had been in and out of it since I was in high school. Always wanting to be on the move and always turning my head back toward it when Trans-Amerika would become more than I could handle.

I looked to the sky, dark clouds hung heavy, threatening to open up again. I remembered Fort Dodge, Iowa...

"Get out! Out of my house. I'm not supporting any bums!" My mother had screamed at me, sending me from her farm and down a gravel road at three in the morning. She had simply grown tired of supporting a parasite who kept his packs on her porch, ate her food, smoked his dope and didn't have a job. Harsh, bitter words from both sides, few meant and none forgotten.

I remembered Fort Dodge. An apartment above a drug store owned by the justice of the peace. The apartment was shared with Steve Butler, one of the finest performers I ever met. He could play bass, sax, piano...and the emotions of anyone he met. He was my brother. His pack also read "Trans-Amerika." We traveled together, tripped together, laughed together and were once jailed together.

It was morning, early morning, after a long night. The night had been filled with laughter, music, pipes and a happy sense of sharing. About four in the morning, our guests had left and Steve and I crashed out, wasted and happily stoned from the night's partying.

In the early morning, I woke feeling greasy and filthy and decided to take a relaxing, cleansing bath. I was soaking in the tub and playing with my plastic submarine, feeling warm and comfortable in the water. Looking at the poster of an old girl friend above the tub and sinking the Ivory soap with a well-aimed torpedo from the submarine. Still a little stoned, kind of early morning stoned.

Then I heard a knock, a loud knock, shaking me out of the relaxation of my suds. Jumping up, I pulled a towel around myself and headed for the door.

"You! Kenneth Lyftogt?" I heard as I opened the door.

"Yeah, what's up?" I gasped, looking out the door at three uniformed cops and two men in dark suits.

"Police. We've got a warrant to search this apartment on suspicion of drugs, stolen goods, arms and desecrated flags."

"Yeah, well," I stuttered, looking behind me at the water pipe on the kitchen table, it's brass bowl filled with weed.

"I didn't steal anything, man, honest," I said, closing the door to a crack between us. I looked into the living room and the flag-covered coffee table, the doorway between the living room and the bedroom was covered with a large flag. "Look, man, a dude flopped here last night. His name's not on that thing. Can I send him home?"

"Forget it, kid," said the detective in an impatient voice. "We saw his name on the mailbox. We're coming in."

They came in, pushing me into the living room, laughing as I pulled on a pair of jeans and threw on a sweater. I looked at them as they began their search, tearing posters down, emptying jars of beads onto the table. I felt an empty sense of disbelief, as if I were in a play written for someone else.

Steve came out of the bedroom, naked, his long, black hair falling down on his shoulders, his hands rubbing his eyes.

I looked at him as he hurriedly tugged on a pair of jeans. His name wasn't on the goddamned warrant, why should he have to be in trouble too? He didn't need this at all. He was planning on getting married soon and earning a living as a musician or as a manager of the store he was working in.

He had never fully rejected Amerika. He had the means and desired to make it in conventional society. To him, Trans-Amerika wasn't his life, just a small section of it. He could drift in and out of the life of Trans-Amerika as casually as he could roll a number. Now a police record would change that, a conviction for dope and flag desecration would put the stamp of Trans-Amerika on him forever.

"Hey, man, what's up?" he nervously shook the words from his mouth.

"We're busted, man," I sighed.

"You said you were busted, I heard you!" The detective said eagerly. "Are we going to find anything, Ken?"

I looked into the kitchen where a cop was searching a table. He accidently knocked over the water pipe, set it back up and proceeded to search a cereal box, ignoring the spilled contents of the pipe.

I looked back at the detective and said, "I don't know."

However, after an hour's search, they managed to find three lids, one BB pistol and thirty-two flags. We had flags on jackets, a flag vest, a flag on my pack, flag sashes and a lot of flag stickers stuck upside down on the door and walls. That's not counting the curtain and the table cloth.

The second man in a suit wasn't a detective like the first, but a newspaper reporter. He had heard my name over the police radio and remembered me from the many demonstrations I had helped organize which he covered.

I remembered him too. I remembered him taking pictures and cheering a man for setting fire to the coffin I had put on the lawn of the Federal building in memory of Jeff Miller, one of the murdered students at Kent State. The coffin was one of four that a small group of people symbolicly marched for four miles after the deaths in Ohio. I remembered the reporter taking my picture as I helped carry Jeff Miller's casket. After taking my picture, he had quickly held up four fingers, then closed his fist. It meant: National Guard four, students nothing. To him, four deaths were a football score and his team was ahead.

Now he was watching another contest. The score seemed to be Fort Dodge police, two, Trans-Amerika nothing. This was the first dope raid the police had made on a Fort Dodge apartment, and he wanted to be a part of it.

He looked at Steve and pointed to one of the upside down flags and asked, "Why are they upside down?"

Steve looked at him and grinned, "distress signal."

"You in distress?" asked the reporter.

Steve's eyes looked at the pile of evidence, then at the ceiling. "Oh, yeah," he sighed.

I burst into a laugh. It seemed so funny. Yeah, we were in distress all right.

The detective grabbed me by the neck and said, "You'll laugh, kid, oh, you'll think it's really funny when you're in front of a judge! Yeah, you punk, you'll laugh at this country and this badge in jail, won't you? Well, won't you, you goddamn punk!" He shouted and shoved me toward the door.

"Hey, should we take these too?" asked a cop, holding up an odd assortment of pipes, knives, papers and beads.

"Yeah, everything. Come on, let's get 'em out of here," shouted the detective.

"I want a souvenir," said the reporter taking a flag sash from the wall.

They let us finish dressing and took us to the city jail and booked us.

"How do you spell marijuana? asked the desk sergeant stuck with filling out the forms.

"D-O-P-E" piped in Steve, eagerly, like a tart in a whore house parlor, trying to please. I laughed at the sarcasm but was cut short by the sergeant's scowl directed our way.

We were taken into the cell block. I saw bars, bars all around. The ceiling was bars, the walls were bars, the door was bars. I looked at them and then at Steve.

"Well, Kenny, I think we did it," he said, looking around.

"Yeah, man, uh, like I'm sorry I got you into this. The mother-jumping warrant was for me, not you." I said, feeling afraid and responsible.

"That's O.K., man," he said. "You got a grand for bail?"

"No way, man," I said. "A grand," I thought. I'd never seen that much money in my life. There was no one I could call for money, no way to raise it myself. A friend had gotten me a lawyer, who found out what the bail was. I was told that a thousand dollars was not much for two felonies, but it seemed monsterous to me.

I looked at Steve, wondering how he would do. His family was quite well off and influential in the community. However, they didn't approve of his moving in with me, saying I would get him into trouble. I was afraid that they would refuse to help him now.

"How about you?" I asked.

"I think my old man will spring for me. I should be out soon."

"I hope so, Steve," I said. "The lawyer said we go to court Monday. Why did we have to get nailed Saturday morning? Man, that's two days before we find out anything."

"That will teach us to throw parties on Friday," said Steve.

"Yeah, I guess so," I said, looking at him, "so no more parties on Fridays." I began to laugh at the feeble joke and Steve joined in with a mild chuckle.

I grew serious when I said, "I guess it don't really matter that the lawyer was talking about two and a half years."

The next morning, Steve was out. No goodbye, nothing. They just woke him up, called him out of the cell and he was gone.

Sunday was a long day. As I lay there in the cell, I thought of the future. Two years meant a big prison, a life I wasn't ready for, an existance for which my life in Trans-Amerika hadn't prepared me. I looked up at the bars and thought of the highway, of mountains, of oceans, of my packs. "I should never have stayed in this town," I thought, "never should have gotten the pad."

Two months ago, I had been in Salt Lake City working in a warehouse, feeling fine and now I was laying on a metal bunk in a Fork Dodge jail. "Never should have stayed here!"

Another prisoner poked his head into my cell. His face covered with bruises and dried blood, his hair matted with dried blood, his chest was taped in bloody adhesive to protect two broken ribs. Two nights earlier, the police had accidently put a prisoner meant for the mental hospital in Cherokee into the same cell with this man. The mental patient had taken a broom stick left by the cops and beaten the man unconscious in an effort to force him to perform fellatio and sodomy on him.

"Kid, can you fight?" asked the bloody man.

"No," I said, feeling small and helpless. "That ain't my thing."

"Well, kid, they got you on a felony. That's the pen, you'll learn there or they'll turn you into a girl."

I looked at him. The bruises and the bandages frightened me. "So I'll learn to fight," I said, turning back to the bars. "For flowers," I thought. "For flowers, I'm in a goddamn cage." I began to laugh, lightly to myself. It was all so completely stupid.

That night, I slept dreaming of Trans-Amerika. I saw myself sitting on the edge of a highway, my thumb going up to meet a new friend. I saw myself walking through a town at the foot of a mountain. I was flying through Amerika, leaving everything ugly behind me, looking forward to love and beauty somewhere down the road that stretched out in front of me.

Whap! The cop's club smashed against the bars next to my head, waking me to Monday morning. The club and the morning erased the memories of highways and mountains, bringing back the jail cell reality.

I was escorted into the courtroom, a cop on each arm. The room was full for this morning's business. I wasn't the only one set for hearing that day, just the only one taken out of jail. I gasped as I saw my mother and brother hurrying over to me. The bitter memories of the ugly night were washed away as I saw her tear-filled eyes. She wanted to do as she had always done--rescue her child from whatever trouble he might be in. Now, in this trouble, she could do absolutely nothing.

I suddenly felt sorry for her. She cared for me. She cared for me very much. It seemed so unfair, that while watching Saturday night television, she had to find out that her son was in jail.

"They wouldn't let me see you," she cried. Her face was wet with tears, but she stood proud. She had dressed in her best for the occasion, her hair was fixed and she had a look of determination about her. No judge would ever be able to tell his cronies that she didn't care enough about her child to leave the factory where she worked to help her son in any way she could. She was right here to help me. She didn't know what to do, but if she could do anything at all, she stood ready.

"They wouldn't let me see you either," said my younger brother. He had left school to see me, to try in his way to help. "One girl even said she was your wife, but they wouldn't let her see you," he added. "They said your kind didn't deserve visitors."

"Yeah, I guess," I said, turning back to my mother. "Don't worry, I'll be all right." I wanted her to leave. She was hurt so much. I got myself into this and I didn't want the stigma to become part of her.

"Ken," she said, "they'll drop the charges. I talked to the D.A., and he'll drop the charges if you join the service."

"Ma, don't you know better?" I pleaded. "That's the

kind of surrender they want. I didn't treat their flag right, I smoke dope and they'll punish me for it, any way they can--in jail or in the army.''

"O.K.," she said, "We've fought about that too much, and I won't fight anymore. Maybe I'm wrong, but it's you they'll put in jail.''

"Yeah, I know," I sighed.

"Look," she said, "Steve said he'd go in if he could join the Air Force, that's not like the Army.''

"Yeah, I could drive a bomber," I said, looking around for Steve. "Ma, Steve had no reason being mixed up in this. If he wants out that way then that's fine. But I won't go into any part of it.''

I saw Steve standing in a corner. His hair was cut and he was dressed in a dark blue suit. He turned to me and waved. I raised my fist in response. I looked at his clothes, then down at my dirty jeans, boots and sweater, all smelling of a weekend in a hot cell.

The judge entered and our hearing began. That particular hearing did nothing but bind us over for a grand jury indictment and transferred me from the city jail to the county jail.

* * * * *

It had been a year since the bust, and now I was walking along a Minnesota highway, looking up to the dark skies and back to the none too bright past. Actually, things really hadn't worked out so bad for us.

The marijuana laws changed in Iowa from a felony to an indictable misdemeanor. Steve had been put on a probation that would leave his record clear of any convictions if he stayed clean for a year. I had been convicted of possession of marijuana and sentenced to thirty days in jail. The sentence was suspended, and I was put on a year's probation with parole terms, meaning I had to have a job and an apartment. I had to be home by midnight and two a.m. on weekends. I could not leave the county without permission from the sheriff, and I was forbidden to engage in any political activity.

They'd dropped the flag charges to save the expense of a trial, a trial they weren't sure they would win. It was a far cry from the two and a half years in jail that the lawyer had originally predicted, and I felt lucky to be spared the time.

For three months, I had adhered to the rules of my probation, but Trans-Amerika was too much a part of me for me to just live and work in Fort Dodge. By mid-winter I was again on the move, freezing in blizzards in Utah and Arizona. By spring, I was engaging in political activity by organizing for and taking part in the May Day demonstrations in Washington, D.C.

I didn't think of the probation again as Trans-Amerika and I became one once more. Now I was looking up at a cloudy sky in Minnesota, remembering a town and some people, anxious to see them again.

I kicked the dust of the gravel road as I walked. The rain had stopped long before. The sun returned, and the road dried to dust at my feet. I looked at the cows in the pasture, their brown eyes staring dumbly at me, the bravest standing at the fence, the rest running to a safe distance. I waved and called out to them, and the brave one retreated to the safety of the rest of the herd.

The farm house where my mother and stepfather lived was just a mile or so down the road. The sky was bright, and I could see the two pine trees that marked the entrance to their drive. I looked forward to the visit. I hoped the old hostilities had been submerged for awhile at least, by time and distance. I didn't want to live here or even stay for a long time. I just wanted to be here for now, for today, and try to feel the roots I had attempted to sever so long ago.

I figured both she and the old man were working, and I would just squat on the front steps and wait. The sun was starting its way down, so the wait wouldn't be long.

I opened the old, squeaky gate, a part of the vine-covered fence circling the small yard. I heard a bark from inside the house, and I knew it was Baby.

Baby was my mother's small toy Manchester dog. A lovable, nervous, completely useless animal that I loved as much as my mother did. I called out, and the dog must have recognized my voice, because the barking became louder and more excited.

"Kenny? Is that you?" A voice from inside the house called. The front door opened, and my mother came out. She was wearing a pair of dark slacks and a colorful top of blue flowering pattern. Her curious face broke into a smile when she saw me standing there. In my shabby clothes, tangled hair and packs, I must have looked like something any mother would refuse to claim. But she smiled and hurried down the steps. "Christ, it really is you, Ken!"

I flung my packs aside and raced to meet her. We embraced on the bottom step as Baby barked at my heels.

"Hi, old girl," I said when she let me go. "And Hi to you too, you little animal," I laughed as I picked up the excited dog. "Hey, Mom, how are you? Really, you're looking good. It's great to see you! Aren't you working anymore? I expected to wait."

"Well, come on inside, Ken. I was just starting dinner, and, yes, I still have my job, but it's Sunday," she said, taking my arm and escorting me into the living room.

"Sunday, huh? Well, I never could get time straight. Really, it's so good to see you again. I've missed you," I said, feeling like a kid home from summer vacation.

"I know, I've missed you too. You could write your mother now and then, you know," she said as she took me into the kitchen where my stepfather sat at the table reading the paper. "Hey, look what just blew in off the road--our own tumble weed!"

"Hello, Ken" he said, holding out his hand. "How are you?"

"Fine, fella, just fine," I said and took his hand.

My stepfather wasn't a bad man at all. In fact, in many ways he was a very good man. But my mother had married him when I was fourteen, and I had always resented him. I guess there was no reason for me to resent him. I had hated my own father with a passion for many years and was happy when mother left him. In fact, when I last saw my real father, he had thrown me out after a brief fist fight that he lost because he was too drunk to stand up. I had left, and my mother and brother and sister left too. Instead of me taking over as "man of the house," my mother had quickly remarried, and I was deposed before I even had a chance to reign.

I felt a lot of bitterness in my new-found status as oldest stepson. That bitterness prevented me from recognizing my mother's need for happiness. I resented her for having brought him into "our" lives. She, in turn, became defensive about her own needs. As a result, the three years we lived together were filled with constant quarrels and a persistant mood of repressed hatred from all sides.

I still had little to say to him. The resentment was still there, less noticeable on both our parts, but still very much a part of our separate realities. I had come to Iowa to see my mother, and he was simply there with her, not in the way, but not really a part of my visit. I could see him or not see him and not be much affected either way. He felt the same toward me. We both knew that our relationship had never been a father-son type and now was no time to try to straighten out a few years of hostilities.

"Well, sit down, Ken. Tell us where you've been," my mother said, motioning me to a chair.

I sat down, relaxed in the wooden kitchen chair and gazed at the familiar surroundings. The simple decorations of a farm kitchen, the calendar on the wall, and the knick knacks on various shelves gave the place a peaceful, comfortable feeling. As I sat there beginning to relax, my stepfather left his place at the table, went into the living room and turned on the television. I watched him go and felt a kind of relief. I knew I should ask him to stay and join the conversation, but his presence made us both nervous. He wasn't a stupid man, and he knew how I felt coming home after all this time. It wasn't easy for me to be in this kitchen, in this house with nothing more to show for my life since I left than a ragged pack and damp bedroll.

As I watched him silently leave the room, I felt like thanking him, and I knew I couldn't do it. A moment of understanding on our part could not erase a lot of years of hate and resentment. Maybe some other time, the mutual tension might be lifted, but now when we were together, we both felt the strain. He did his part to relieve it by simply leaving the room, and I hoped he knew that in my own silent way, I appreciated it.

"Ken, are you back for good?" My mother asked in a light, curious tone that hid her seriousness.

I looked at her as she lit a cigarette. To me, she looked the same as she always had. My earliest memories were of her chopping wood for the stove that heated our little tar paper shack she and my father had built. I thought of her scrubbing our clothes in a large washtub in back of the house, or hoeing

seemingly endless rows of tomatoes, and in the fall, canning
the vegetables she raised. It seemed strange to me that she
looked no different now. She was well into middle age now,
and when she was not much older than I, she was rearing
three babies in the middle of a Minnesota forest.

It had taken me a long time to realize the inner strength
she had. It had been that strength that sustained her through
the years of poverty and neglect that were the largest part of
her marriage. She had virtually reared her children alone
because of their father's indifference to his role of husband
and father. All those years, I had spent growing up, making
emotional and monetary demands on her and not realizing
the strain she was under. She had only herself to turn to in
those years. There was no one to comfort her when she was
sick or weary, no one to reassure her about the brightness of
the future. Only herself. I looked at her and hoped her
strength would continue to sustain her because her oldest
son didn't have any idea of where he was going and could not
be a source of strength for her.

"No, Mom," I answered. "I won't be staying. I was just
passing north of here, and I thought I'd stop in for a visit.
Can I bum one of those?" I added, pointing to her cigarettes.

"Well, I really wish you'd stay. Iowa isn't really so bad,
you know." She passed me the pack and a lighter.

"No, Mom," I said, "it's not the state or even the town.
It's me. I don't have any reason to stay anymore. No matter
where I land, I feel that I gotta' get going again."

"What do you need to make you settle down?" she
asked, putting her hand over mine. "You know I don't care
anymore about money than you. I understood when I heard
you gave up that job in Des Moines. I understood leaving a
lot of money if you weren't happy at it. But what I don't
understand is what you gave it up for."

"I don't know, Mom, I really don't." I said. "That job
certainly wasn't any reason to settle down. I came to Iowa
and was told I could make good money managing that
restaurant. Maybe I could have, but money just didn't seem
to be a good reason to give up the highway. That's all that job
offered me; money, not any sort of life, so I kept going."

"And what about that girl?" she asked. "The one who
went to Washington with you. Did she have anything to do
with it?"

"I don't know, Mom," I said. "It hurt when she split, it really did. We got back together in Oakland for a while, but there was nothing left. I guess I was pretty happy with her. I thought if I followed her, things might work out, but they didn't, so I kept moving. That's all I was doing when I met her in the first place, just moving. The job, the money, they were just interruptions. Maybe she was just an interruption too. So now I'm just moving again." I finished and sat back in my chair, nervously fingering my wristband, feeling almost guilty about saying so much, wondering what her reaction to my confession would be.

"Kenny," she said softly, "do you know what day next Thursday is?"

I grinned. "I'm sorry, I don't. This is July, isn't it? I mean, I may lose track of the days, but please don't tell me I lost the whole month too!"

She laughed, "No, kid, you're right, it's July, and Thursday, you'll be twenty years old." Then her voice became serious and she said, "You're not a child anymore, Ken, and you're doing the same thing now that you were doing two, three years ago. School was just an interruption too, but you'd better start thinking of the future and face it; someday, responsibility is going to hit you, and you won't know how to handle it."

"That's just it, Mom, I don't know how to handle it. When things get rough, I can't handle it, and I leave. Maybe I could have handled the parole, but I left it. Maybe I could be a success in a restaurant, but I left it. I left those things and a hundred others that you don't know about.

"It's not that I'm looking for anything, Mom," I continued. "I'm not. The image of the existential searcher doesn't make it with me. I'm not looking for anything. I don't look forward to what might happen tomorrow. I just remember yesterday. It's the whole bit, really. Just feeling sorry for myself and looking for a way to forget."

"Remember when you threw me out because of what I am? Well, I sometimes feel like doing it myself. Shit, Mom, there's a whole world out there; things happening but I'm just waiting to hear about it when somebody picks me up."

"Kenny," she said, putting out her cigarette and looking at me. Her eyes shone, soft loving, trying hard to understand. It was strange that for so long, I took that love for granted. I had even denied its existence many times. Now, I looked at her and knew that it had always been there.

"I guess I could tell you all the things that are wrong with you," she said, "but you already know and can explain them better than I. So all I'll do is tell you that you've got a home here anytime you want to settle down. O.K.?"

I nodded and looked down at my hands and the unlit cigarette in my fingers. Tears formed in my eyes, and I couldn't look up. She had no ideas or ways to magically put a sense of responsibility into my head, but she still told me she would be there to help me in any way she could, any time I needed it.

"Hey, boy of mine," she said, brightening up and lightly slapping the top of my head, "I've got to finish dinner, so why don't you clean up. I bet it's been awhile."

"Yeah," I laughed, "a couple of days. I'll get my gear in order first." I went outside and unrolled my bedroll and hung it and the blanket over the clothesline to dry out from drenching that morning. I took my leather jacket and my pack inside, draped the jacket over a chair and threw the pack in a corner, after taking out a clean pair of socks and a clean shirt.

The long, soaking bath felt so good. I lay there, covered with white lather and draped my legs over the side. I thought of where I would go from here. I didn't know, but I knew I couldn't stay. My mother had been glad to see me, but if I stayed in her house, a lot of bitterness would be bound to develop again. I decided that the next day, I would go into town and see Steve and a few other people, then be on my way.

Later, we were all sitting around the table, having a fine meal. Like any "traditional" mother, mine could cook and right about then, the roast beef and whipped potatoes went down so very fine that I could almost hear my stomach and whole body thanking me.

"How long are you going to hang around?" asked my stepfather over a cup of coffee. He didn't sound sarcastic, just curious.

"I don't know." I answered. "I want to see Steve and see if he's still planning on getting married. Then I guess I'll be going. Tomorrow or the next day."

"Well," he muttered, "I could probably help you find work if you want to stay."

"Thanks, really, thanks a lot, but I just stopped in for a visit," I said. I knew that in his way, he wanted to help too.

"Steve's not here anymore," my mother said.

"What? Why?" I asked, startled.

"He stopped in a week ago," she said. "He lost his job at the shoe store a couple of months ago. He said that he couldn't find work here, so he left town to look. As far as I know, he's still going to marry that girl, but I don't know when."

"I wonder how Mel is taking that," I thought, then asked my mother, "Do you know Melody Vincent, his girlfriend?"

"I've never met her," she answered. "Do you know her very well?"

"We've had a couple of pretty good talks, but I really don't know her that well," I said. "Does Steve have any idea where to look? She's straight as hell and she could be really upset with him just taking off."

"Oh, yeah," she said. "I guess he's got some kind of construction work lined up in Denver. He was pretty excited about it. He likes Denver."

"Yeah, I know," I said, "We went there together awhile back. Well, at least he's not wandering around looking for a job. Mel should understand that. She knows they need money to get married, and construction work pays well."

The meal was finished and I actually enjoyed washing the dishes as Mom and I talked about absolutely nothing. It was a pleasant evening, all in all, a soft kind of reunion just as I had hoped it would be.

That night, I threw back the blankets on my bed. I smiled at the sight of clean sheets. It was going to be a long night's sleep, and in the morning I would be on my way in some direction.

*****

My feet felt cool, the swiftly flowing water of the brook cooled them as the ripples splashed and played over, under, around and through my heels and toes resting bare in the water. My head lay back resting on the flag of my pack, and I looked up into the tall Wisconsin trees. My boots and socks lay on the grass next to me. It had been a hot day, it was now mid-afternoon, the cool of the evening hadn't really begun, but the blazing heat of the day had ended.

I smiled to myself as I lay there cooling my feet in the brook. For the last couple of weeks, I had been slowly drifting around the Midwest. I had worked as a cook for a couple of days in Sioux City, and in Des Moines, I ran into a paranoid freak who had given me almost a quarter pound of pretty good dope. Now, with a few dollars and a fine stash, I was just on the Wisconsin side of the Wisconsin-Minnesota border deciding where to go from here.

I reached into my pocket for my papers and dope. The papers were brightly colored flags and made a nice looking number. I looked up at the sound of footsteps on the pavement of the nearby road. The steps left the road, and I began to hear twigs breaking, the leaves rustling. I put the paraphernalia back and looked toward the sound.

There was what I had expected to see--the uniform of a highway patrolman.

"Hello there, sir," I said, sitting up. "What's up?"

"Hello to you, son. Where are you going?" he answered.

"Uh-uh, Minneapolis."

"Mmm, nice city. Where are you coming from?"

"Rock Island and Davenport," I said.

"Well, son," he said, "let me see some I.D., please."

I handed him the draft card I never got around to burning, which worked out quite well since I didn't drive and it was a pretty good I.D.

He took it and continued, "What are the hitchhiking laws, son?"

"Well, sir, it depends on the states," I said. "Most states say no to standing on the interstate, but that's cool in some. I just try to make it a rule to be on the ramps."

"Good rule," he said. "This is Wisconsin, and it's worth quite a stiff fine if I catch you on the interstate. I just caught a kid from your home town last week and took him in for just that reason."

"Really," I looked up, interested. "Somebody from Fort Dodge. Who? Maybe I know him."

"His name was Steve Butler," he said. "He was fined thirty dollars."

"Jesus," I gasped and thought to myself, "What the Sam Hell is he doing here? He's supposed to be working in Denver." "Uh, sir," I said. "Did he tell you where he was going? Did he pay his fine or is he serving a hitch of some sort?''

"Do you know him?'' the patrolman asked.

"Yeah,'' I muttered, "I know him.''

"Well, some people from Winona bailed him out an hour after I brought him in,'' he said.

"Thanks, guy,'' I said as he motioned me to follow him to the patrol car.

Barefoot, I hopped over the brook and across the leaves and twigs of this little patch of forest.

I leaned against the car as he made a quick check on me. Those checks generally worried me even though I averaged about one a day. I always feared that someday the Webster County Sheriff would decide to tell his fellow minions of the law that I jumped my parole. So far though, he hadn't. Right then, however, I wasn't thinking of myself. I forgot about the dope in my pocket and the possibility of a bust.

"What was Steve doing here in Wisconsin? Why wasn't he working where he was supposed to be? Wasn't he going to be married? Why didn't he even have enough for his own bail?'' I thought as the patrolman finished his check.

"O.K., son,'' he said, "you're clean. In Wisconsin, stay on the ramps.''

"Thanks, man,'' I answered. "Uh, how far is Winona from here?''

"About forty miles on this highway,'' he said, pointing west.

I thanked him again and watched him drive away. I went back to my gear and put my socks and boots on. I sat there thinking of what I should do. I figured I knew who in Winona had sprung Steve. Maybe they could answer a few questions for me.

I walked along the highway, slowly rolling a number, looking for cars that weren't there and wondering if Steve was in some kind of trouble. The only person that I knew of in Winona who would put up money for him was one of his ex-girlfriends who was doing a little college time there. I lit the number and turned west on the highway.

Hiding the number in my palm, I thumbed a car and it pulled over for me. Gathering up my gear, I ran toward it, the dope still smoking between my fingers. I looked inside the car and saw a freak, a roach clip earring in his left ear and a pair of yellow wire-rimmed glasses. His long dark hair was tied back in a ponytail.

"Here, man, hold this," I said, handing him the joint. He took it with a wide smile, and I threw my gear in the back.

"Where you going?" I asked as I crawled into the front seat.

"Winona, man," he said, holding his hand out, thumb held high, ready to receive the hand clasp of Trans-Amerika. "Thanks for the weed. I'm out."

I laughed, taking his hand. "Winona's where I'm going too, so let's get loaded."

"I can dig that," he said and pointed to the glove compartment. "Check out the glove compartment. There's an orange and a white tab in the aspirin bottle. Help yourself to either. The orange is acid, the white's supposed to be mesc."

"Thank you, man, I'll take the orange," I said, shaking the tablet out of the bottle. I took out my wallet and a piece of paper. I didn't feel like tripping just yet, but a free hit was hard to pass up. I wrapped it in paper and slipped it between two pictures in my wallet. "Is this other bottle empty for good, or are you going to use it for something special?" I asked, holding up a similar aspirin bottle that was next to the first.

"No, that just had Anacin in it," he said. "I ran out, that's all. Why?"

"Here's why," I grinned, and quickly filled the bottle with weed.

"Why'd you do that?" he laughed.

"Why not? It was given to me. If I hold much more than a lid, I get paranoid, so here." I answered and flipped the bottle into the glove compartment and closed the door.

"Thanks a lot," he said. "I'm Karl."

"I'm Kenny," I said, and I started to roll another number. "Where you from, Karl?"

"I'm from LaCrosse, but I live in Ames, Iowa," he answered. "Where you from?"

"Iowa, too," I said and lit the number.

"Far out! What's in Winona?"

"I've got to see someone," I said and sat far back in the seat, taking a deep hit on the number, thinking of Steve and hoping that his plans of love had not been shattered. I didn't

want his life destroyed, his future ruined, because of a
faltering romance. Steve had never been fully a part of
Trans-Amerika, his path back to respectability had always
been too important for him to give up. Now, he had
apparently thrown that path away, and I had to find out why.
Steve had been too good a friend for me to simply keep
moving and ignore the questions I had about him.

For the next half hour, Karl and I laughed, exchanged
stories of travels and dope and just before the sun went
down, he let me off in downtown Winona.

"What was her last name?" I thought. Her folks lived
here too, and I figured she was living with them. She and
Steve had broken up in a friendly sort of way a little over a
year ago when she moved here. She had given me her
address in case I came up this way. Unfortunately, I lost the
address long ago and now I sat on my pack just outside a
phone booth, trying to remember her last name.

"Von Helsing!" I thought. "Right! Just like in
'Dracula.' How could I forget it? I'd even teased her about
it."

I quickly looked up the address and collared a passerby
for directions. All my life I had hated talking on the phone,
so, to me, phone books were just sources of addresses.

The passerby not only gave me directions, he gave me a
ride to the door. He was a mild-mannered college student. I
thanked him by handing him a joint. He turned a bit red, but
silently accepted the weed. I laughed to myself as I
approached the door.

I threw my gear onto the lawn and rang the doorbell.

Rubbing my hair, I nervously asked the woman who
answered the door, "Hello, ma'am. Uh, is Barbara at
home?" I was stoned and trying to act straight. If this wasn't
serious, I would have started laughing in a second.

"No, she's not here now. Who are you?" she asked me.
She looked at me suspiciously, and I could see why. She was
standing in the doorway of her suburban home with its
freshly mowed lawn in front. She was dressed in a
good-looking light pant suit. Her hair showed she'd recently
visited a good beauty shop. I, on the other hand, was wearing
dusty boots, patched jeans, a blue work shirt, red scarf and
my packs were next to me on her good-looking lawn.

"Well, ma'am, I'm a friend of Steve Butler's just passing

through, and I--well...Ma'am, did Barb get him out of the jug in Wisconsin?'' I asked, pointing east.

''Oh,'' she said, brightening up. ''You're a friend of Steve? Please come in.'' She motioned me inside where we sat down at the kitchen table, and she poured a large glass of lemonade for me. ''No, Barb didn't bail out Steve. Her father and I did. She's in California visiting her boyfriend.''

I looked at the spotless porcelain kitchen, its shiny waxed floors, and into the living room to the thick, ankle-deep carpet and large television. I took a deep drink of my lemonade and felt even more stoned, but managed to ask, ''Did you talk to Steve? I mean, what's he doing here? Did he say he was going to be married?''

''No, he didn't,'' she said, suddenly looking more serious. ''He said he was just traveling around and decided to come and visit Barb.''

''And he didn't mention his old lady--I mean, the girl he was going to marry?'' I asked.

''Not a word. He had a meal with us, promised he'd pay the money back as soon as possible and left.''

I nodded and thought to myself about the way I always took off if love didn't work out right. ''Did Mel leave him?'' I thought. ''Is he just throwing everything away because she left him? Maybe he got scared and left her?'' I didn't know, but it was obvious that something had happened--something serious enough to make him take up residence in Trans-Amerika. And I had better find out what.

''Did he tell you where he was going when he left?'' I asked.

''No, I'm sorry,'' she answered. ''I took it for granted that he had gone back home. I mean, where can you go without any money?''

I smiled inside and answered her, ''You're right. I think he went back to Fort Dodge.'' I stood up, my stoned mind reeling, wondering what was going on. I knew that I'd better head back to Fort Dodge and get some of these questions answered.

''Thank you, ma'am,'' I said. ''I appreciate it. I'll be going now.''

''That's fine,'' she said. ''Would you like to stay for dinner or something? It's after six.''

I looked down at my boots, which were covered with dust and standing on her thick carpet. "No thanks, ma'am, it's still early."

"All right, have a nice trip. Sorry I couldn't help you any more," she said as I threw my gear over my shoulder and started to walk away. I waved, and she waved and watched me leave.

Once on the highway, I lit a number and waited for a car to come by. I really couldn't imagine Steve aimlessly drifting. True, his packs also read "Trans-Amerika," but even when he traveled with me, he was always very conscious of when he had to be "home" and back at "work." Something really must have happened to send him traveling down a highway, broke and wandering, telling no one anything about why. I took a long hit and tried to figure out why. I knew that if any answers could be found, they would be found in Fort Dodge.

CHILDREN

"Fort Dodge again," I thought as I walked along its main street. The sun was just going down, and the endless stream of cars was once again driving up and down the street. Boys looking to get laid, girls looking for boys, and having what the boys were looking for. Lights from bars advertising their wares--"The Hungry Eye-Go-Go Nightly--Adults Only"---"The Flame--Drink Schlitz." Headlights from cars, flashing in signals to friends. New cars, old cars, all filled with high school kids free for the summer, free from school, driving the street looking for high school friends. A biker passed me, seeing my packs, he waved. I looked at his patch; Banshees-Iowa. Somehow, it seemed strange to see an outlaw biker in Iowa.

I had taken my time getting here from Winona. I didn't know why I was here at all. Someone was hurt, somehow Steve was in trouble, in some way his life had fallen apart. I didn't know if it was just curiosity or an urge to help. The confusion in my mind had slowed me down on my way here in the ten hour trip that took two days. Two days I had spent partying in Mankato and Albert Lea, trying to decide what I was going to do once I made it to Fort Dodge. Now I was here, and as confused as I was two days earlier. I threw my gear on the sidewalk and leaned against a city parking meter. I reached into my pocket for a number and matches. Steve's parents didn't live here anymore, so the only person I could think to contact would be Mel. Maybe she had some answers. If she didn't know anything, then I would know that Steve's head was really messed up.

"What then?" I thought. "What if she doesn't know where he is? What if she don't know nothin'? What then? Do I try to find him? Do I just call it a day? Jesus, Kenny!" I cursed to myself, "It's his goddamn life! What help could you be, anyway? Why don't you just get the hell out of this town, out of this state and stop looking for trouble, especially someone else's trouble?"

I took a deep drag on the number, instinctively looking

around for Fort Dodge police. "Yeah, forget the whole thing," I thought, "and get out of here."

"Kenny--Hey, Kenny!"

I quickly ate the joint as I turned looking for the person calling my name. A car pulled over to the curb, and a shaggy-headed freak in a tie-dyed T-shirt jumped out. The shirt was dyed red and blue, red on top, blue on the bottom, and a large yellow star in the middle--a Viet Cong flag.

"Denny," I shouted, and we both ran to meet each other. He was looking more worn than I remembered. Denny was a hard-nosed politico. There hadn't been a demonstration in Iowa that he hadn't laid a helping hand to. There wasn't an Iowa politician, local or national that didn't show a respect for his organizational abilities. Lately, though, his life had seemed aimless. His marriage had fallen apart, and his draft board had grabbed him. It was for their benefit that he had built the Viet Cong shirt (Victor Charlie). He was momentarily out of their clutches as a security risk. Last I heard, he was working a job that he hated. For him, politics had ended, and his future was as questionable to him as to anyone else. His eyes, sparkling in recognition, still reflected a deep sadness. His tall body seemed to stoop, and his appearance betrayed a lack of upkeep that he usually wouldn't have let happen.

"Ken, how are you? Where you been? When did you get back in town?" he asked in one excited breath.

I threw my gear into the back of his car, we both hopped in and he started driving. "Just looking at the Pacific, man," I answered.

"Here, fella'," he said, throwing me a lid, "you roll. I take it you didn't take the big money in Des Moines."

"No, I split to Oakland. Shit, man, can you imagine me with money?" And we both began to laugh. I pulled out my papers and started to roll.

"What about your old lady in California? I guess that's why you went there, wasn't it?" he asked, throwing me a book of matches.

"Well, we didn't get it on at all, and I split. She was glad I did, I guess. It was her pad anyway. Besides, I wasn't what she wanted, and we both knew it." I lit the pot and took a long pull, holding the smoke deep in my lungs as Denny spoke again.

"Yeah, man, I know how that is." His face took on a momentary look of sorrow. "Hey, dude, you got any plans?" he asked, brightening up.

"No, none. Why?" I answered.

"Well, 'Wire' is playing in Dakota City tonight, and I was just headed up to hear them. They're pretty good."

"Far out, man," I said. "I can dig it. I haven't seen a concert for awhile!"

"Sorry I don't have anything but weed to offer," he said, taking his turn on the number. "I just did my last hit of mesc, and I'm waiting to get off. Everything around here is really speedy lately, but not too bad in all."

"Don't worry," I said, remembering my wallet. "I've got a hit of orange goody here." And I produced the acid I had been given two days earlier. I put it on my tongue, and in an instant it was gone, almost as if it had never been there. A sign of really good acid.

"Let's fly, Ken," he said and gunned the car. "We'll be off by the time the concert starts." Any special reason you came back, like are you staying, or what?"

"I'm looking for Steve Butler, Denny. Have you seen him?"

"Not for well over a month. I hitched to Okoboji with him for the Fourth. He wasn't working then, and said he had some construction thing lined up by Denver, and he'd be leaving town for awhile."

"What about Mel? Are they still planning to get married?" I asked.

"Oh, yeah," he said as he pulled into the parking lot of a liquor store. "You got any change?"

"Sure, man" I said, tossing him a few dimes and quarters. In a minute, he was back with a bottle of Ripple wine and continuing on with what he was saying.

"Steve moved the date up quite a bit, but it's still on as far as I know. He closed down his pad, and I'm living there now. So I guess he's still working out there. He hasn't been back here yet, anyway. Why do you ask? Hey, roll another one, and let's drink this shit with it."

"Sure, man," I said, and rolled another number, avoiding his question. I lit the number, taking a long hit, coughed a little at the first rush of the burning paper, then silenced it with the wine.

Half an hour later, my mind was beginning to melt into itself as I stood in line to buy my ticket. I thought of Steve and of the cop in Wisconsin and of the woman with the thick carpet in Winona. "If Mel's expecting to be married, then she thinks the old boy's working in Colorado," I thought, then my mind jumped forward and backwards at the same time. "But he's not, he's gone, he was north of here, not in Colorado where he's supposed to be. If he's not in Denver, and not in Wisconsin or Minnesota or home in Fort Dodge, then where is he? He's gone."

My mind was buzzing from the acid, visions of highways criss-crossing each other played in front of my eyes. At each intersection of the highways was Steve, holding his Trans-Amerika pack in front of him. I bought my ticket and in a daze followed Denny into the darkened ballroom. He was silently losing himself in his own vapors of mescaline. The band was just starting its first song as we sat on the floor. I looked at Denny as he took the last drink of wine. I hadn't noticed him smuggle the bottle into the room. I laughed as he slid the empty container under a booth.

The band was loud, loud, and in my reeling mind, sounding good. I felt each note as I sat back and listened. "A band has a lot of duties to a stoned person," I thought. "They've got to take my trip out of my hands and guide it themselves. They've got to send me places I could never reach by myself. But as well as sending me places, they've got to be able to return me because I didn't get there alone, and I need help to get back."

Denny left the floor, hit on a young blond lady, and started to dance, leaving me alone on the floor.

I lay back, eyes closed, remembering the band's duties. I thought of returning, of getting back from somewhere I'd never been. My mind was flashing and jumping. "Back," I thought. "From where? From where Steve is?"

"Where is Steve?"

"Steve is lost." My mind screamed amid pictures of Steve in the middle of a criss-crossed highway. "Steve is lost--Steve is LOST!!"

"Are you Steve, Ken? Are you lost? You got him thrown in jail; you lost him! You were in jail, same as him; you ARE him! You are lost, Ken; Steve, you are lost!"

My face changed places with his on the criss-crossed

highway. "I'm lost!" I said, grabbing my head as I lay on the floor. "Where am I? Who am I?"

"I'm in Oakland--no, Palo Alto--no, Denver, working construction. I'm going to marry Melody!"

"NO!" I screamed to myself rolling over on the floor. "No! Steve's in Denver, and he's going to be married--not me!"

"Steve's not in Denver; he's lost," my brain screamed to me. "Where are you? Who are you?"

I sat up and shouted back at my brain, "I'm Kenny, not Steve! I'm in--where am I?" My eyes flashed open, and the room was in total darkness except for five glowing silhouettes on stage.

I shook my head violently, the acid splashing colors and pictures all over the inside of my eyes, painting a picture of confusion, Steve, highways, and myself lost among them. The glowing silhouettes were drowned in a colorful sea of confusion.

Something grabbed my shirt and hauled me to my feet. I looked to what it was and saw a badge. The bouncer was talking to me.

"Don't lie on the floor, kid," he said and pushed me backwards. His eyes gave a start when he saw the knife at my belt.

I jumped back at him, madness in my brain, the madness of not knowing who I was or where I was.

"You don't like me, do you, fucker?! Well, do you?!" I screamed at him, my voice all but drowned out by the band.

"I just told you not to lie down," he said, bracing himself for my assault.

Just then, I saw Denny coming toward me, and I calmed myself as I thought, "Denny, yeah, Denny. I'm in Iowa at a concert with Denny." My brain suddenly went silent, for now I knew who I was and where I was. I turned back to the bouncer. "I'll leave if you want me to, if you don't want me to stay, I won't," I said in a voice that was at the same time soft and loud. "If you don't want me to lay down, I won't. Just tell me what to do. I'll do whatever you say."

"That's O.K.," he said. "Sorry I pushed you; just don't lie down. People want to dance here." He slowly backed away from me and out of my sight. At the same time, Denny reached me.

"How you doing, Ken? He giving you trouble?" he asked.

"No, man, it's great. I'm in Iowa." I laughed, "And I know who I am!"

Luckily Denny was off someplace on his own trip, because he didn't try to make sense out of what I just said.

I sat up on the floor, making sure to stay seated and leave plenty of room for the dancers. I looked to where the bouncer went and saw him talking to another bouncer, pointing to me. My mind was clearing, the music was taking control again and bringing me back to the place I left at the command of the melodies. I turned from the bouncer, hoping that there wouldn't be any more hassles from him. I didn't want confusion and challenges coming at me, confronting me, from the outside. Not when there were so many points of confusion within my own head.

The confusion was calm now; however, my agitated, screaming wild brain was drifting into the magic of the music. The band was doing its duty to me so well that I forgot the mad, mental hysteria of a moment earlier. The images still danced and played within me. The criss-crossed highway, Steve, a woman with a porceline kitchen and thick carpet, a Wisconsin policeman with a memory for names. All were there inside me. I could see them, but now I could sort them out and put each in its place, because I knew where I was. The sense of confusion was gone.

A few hours later, the concert ended, and Denny and I silently drove home. The silence was broken only by a few casual remarks about the quality of the night's music and dope.

I settled back in the seat of the car and casually rolled a joint. I looked into the back seat at my gear, the pack with the flag and leather peace symbol and the almost sacred words written on it. I looked at Denny, his hawk-like face intent on the road, his mind lost in private thoughts. "This could be any ride," I thought. "I could be any place in the whole world and things would be pretty much the same." I would be lying back in the car seat with a bag of weed and rolling papers in my hand, wondering about the thoughts inside the head of the driver.

I was in Iowa, a place I had lived quite a few years. I knew where I was because I could relate Denny's face to a hundred

Iowa memories. If it wasn't Denny, though, if it wasn't on old friend driving the car down the highway, what would be the difference? This ride was the same as a hundred or a thousand other rides because I was the same. I was just someone a person gathered up off a highway and was traveling with for awhile. Tomorrow I would be gone, repeating the pattern someplace else.

I wondered if I should feel sad at the realization that I had no reason to feel different now or yesterday or tomorrow. I didn't know how I felt about being constantly the same in a world of constant change. For the moment, I didn't feel anything. I simply accepted it, the same way I accepted the ride and the companionship of the moment.

That night we slept, he in his room and I in my bedroll on the living room floor. Before falling asleep, I thought of Steve, of the confusion he must be feeling as a part of Trans-Amerika. As I thought of Steve, I decided to let him be. I decided to leave and let him live his life as he chose. I knew that I was in no position to give him advice and I had no right to demand an explanation from him just to satisfy my own curiosity.

If someone came to me and demanded to know why I was living like I was--why I gave up certain things for a highway of uncertainty--I knew I could never give them a satisfactory answer. If I knew that I had no answers, how could I expect any from him?

The next day, after a meal and a bath, I gathered my things together and said goodbye to Denny.

"Where are you going from here, Ken?" he asked during the meal.

"Don't know. East, maybe." I answered. "I was slowly heading that way when I came back here."

"Why did you come here, anyway?" he asked. "If you had a reason to come here, you certainly haven't lost it in one night."

"Yeah, Denny, I did lose it," I said. "Steve isn't working in Colorado. I got word that he's not doing much more than I. I came here to see why, that's all. He's not in town, and I don't think I should go looking for him just because I'm curious."

"It must have meant something to you when you came here. Why doesn't it now?"

"I don't know, but it doesn't. I guess I was just wondering if the dope trouble we had was a part of it. His chick is really straight, and he might not have told her. You know what could happen if she found out accidently."

"Yeah, I know," he said as he got up and began to clear away the dishes. "Thanks for fixing dinner. I bet if you wanted to hang around, they'd hire you back at the restaurant."

"Probably, but I just can't seem to get into keeping any sort of schedule," I answered, handing him my plate. "Besides, the last time I came here to work in a restaurant, they expected me to be good manager material. No, I'm through with grills, broilers and stoves. I just want to live day to day and fine people who care about you even if you don't have any responsibility."

"Have you found anything, Ken? Have you found anything better out there? You don't look any different now than you did a year ago. You still look like you're afraid of your own shadow. Are you ducking responsibilities because you really don't want them or because you're afraid you can't handle them? Have you ever really grabbed hold of a problem and wrestled with it until one of you was beaten? Don't answer it," he said, his voice louder and very serious. "I know what you've done. You've hit the road, left the problems behind."

"Look at that pack," he continued, pointing to my gear. "Amerika, it's still Amerika--a war-mongering, capitalist arsenal, and you're wandering around it. Refusing to try to change anything isn't helping you or it at all. I've got the feeling that you've been damaged more by refusing to fight back than you realize."

"O.K., Denny, O.K.," I said. "So what do I do? Build a demonstration? March through streets? Or do I work at a job and make lots of money and vote for the lesser of two evils? Maybe I ain't found anything better out there, but, Jesus, man, what the fuck is there any place else? What has anything got that makes it worthwhile? Makes it worth fighting for?"

"I don't know, man," I continued, "I haven't been in a demonstration for over three months, not counting the fringes of some street fighting in New Mexico. I just don't seem up to it anymore."

"Maybe I shouldn't give you lectures on self confidence, Ken. I'm not doing much of anything myself," Denny said, sitting back down at the table and talking in a soft tone of voice. "I just think you better get involved in something pretty soon, or you'll be in trouble. Know what I mean?"

"Oh, yeah, I do," I answered, "but I can't see anything to get involved in just yet."

Twenty minutes later, I was walking along a Fort Dodge street. Memories were floating through me as I slowly made my way to the eastbound highway. The pack felt heavy, and I looked forward to throwing them in a car and settling back for a nice, long ride.

I looked at the light, it was red and I waited for it to change so I could cross the street. Looking down the street, I thought I recognized the navy blue Corvair coming toward me. I did recognize it. It was owned by Steve's girlfriend. I waved and shouted, "Mel! Hey, Melody!"

"Kenny!" she said, pulling the car over to the curb. I threw my gear into the back seat and crawled in next to her. She was looking good, her light blond hair was softly formed around her delicate, pale face. Her blue eyes were dancing with recognition. Her clothes were designed in bright summer colors, all completely complimenting her hair and eyes.

"How are you, Mel?" I asked excitedly. "You're looking good."

"I'm fine, Ken. What are you doing here? It's been awhile," she answered, reaching over to pat my hand.

"Well," I said nervously, "where are you living, Mel? Are you working anywhere?"

"Come on...I'm going there now. I share a house with three other girls. I'm working as a receptionist now. I'm armed with my trusty telephone and get to talk to bunches of people."

"That's cool," I said, and she drove to a large white house about eight blocks away.

We went inside, and she poured us each a Pepsi. I looked at her as she fixed the drinks. Her hand was empty; the diamond she had worn so proudly for so long was missing.

"Here," she said. "Now, answer me, is there anything special that brings you to Iowa?"

"Uh, no Mel, nothing much, just passing through, sort

of,'' I stammered.

"Ken?'' she began a question and quickly looked down to her glass. She nervously stirred an ice cube with her finger. "Have you seen Steve? I was hoping you had come here to tell me about him.''

"When's the last time you saw him?'' I asked.

She looked up, her lip trembling slightly, her blue eyes shining with half-formed tears. "He went off to the lake with Denny the Fourth of July, then came back a couple of weeks later saying he had a job in Colorado. I didn't even know he was looking for work out of town.''

She quickly sniffed away a sob and rubbed her arm across her eyes. "Anyway, he said he had a good-paying construction job and in a month or so we'd have plenty of money to get married on. So we moved the wedding date up a month. Then he went back to Denver. I haven't seen or heard from him since. I've got the goddamned invitations ready, I've made two payments on the rings, and I don't know where he is, if he's alive or dead or what.'' At that point, she broke down into sobs, both hands to her face, tears running through her bare fingers.

I moved to put my arms around her and let her head fall on my shoulder, but I stopped myself in the middle of the motion. Instead, I lowered my eyes to my glass and its slowly melting ice cube. When she recovered enough to listen, I told her what I'd found out in Wisconsin and Minnesota.

"Then he never had a job in Colorado?'' she asked in a broken voice. "He just wanted to leave me?''

"I don't know, Mel,'' I said. "All I know is as of about two weeks ago, he wasn't in Colorado, and he doesn't have any money. A lot of things could have happened. Anyway, I guess he's just on the move. Running away from the whole thing.'' I took a long drink of Pepsi and waited for her answer.

"So where is he? Why doesn't he let me know what's going on? I could understand if he didn't want to get married. Why the hell couldn't he talk to me about it? What am I supposed to do? What am I supposed to do? What am I supposed to think?'' Her voice was pleading, almost screaming.

I raised the glass to my lips, afraid to answer. It wasn't the kind of question I was familiar with. No one had ever asked me what to do when someone leaves Amerika for a highway. No one I had ever met was crying over the unexplained departure of someone they loved. I finished the drink and looked at her. In her face, in her eyes were the tears and worries of every mother, girlfriend or relative who didn't know if someone they loved was alive or dead.

I looked at her, but she avoided my eyes and wiped the tears from her cheek. "Mel, did you know he was on probation for dope? And did you have a fight about that?"

"No," she said, her face looking down at her fingers as she slowly scratched one of them. "He told me about that." She quickly looked up and said in a hurried voice, "I never blamed you for getting him in trouble, Kenny. I didn't. He told me about how he didn't know the dope was there, but if he didn't hold it against you, I shouldn't either. He was unlucky, sure, but in a year he wouldn't even have a record. So we never had a fight about that. I understood."

"Thanks, Mel," I said with a wink. And I wondered how much she really knew about Steve. He wasn't a hard-core Trans-Amerikan freak then, but he did his share of dope and contributed to the illegal highs with his share of the money.

"Do you have any idea where he is, Ken?"

"No, I don't. I'm sorry," I said.

For the rest of the day, we talked about Steve, about their plans together, about the money troubles he had after he lost his job at the shoe store. She had no idea why he lost the job, but she knew it had bothered him a great deal. She felt a change had come over him after the loss of income. She had attributed the change to worry about the financial status of their impending marriage.

As darkness forced its way into every corner of the sky, I decided to try to find Steve. It was one thing to ignore the question floating around in my mind and yet another to ignore the questions of this girl when her whole life was wrapped up in the man.

The stars were breaking through the summer sky, tiny points of light shining on the darkness. The shadows on the sidewalks made monsters of trees and giants of buildings as I slowly walked. My head was low as I thought of the day and of the terribly afraid and confused lady that I had spent the day with. I wondered why Steve had kept so many things from her. I remembered when he had told me of his plans for marriage. I asked him why he felt he had to be bothered with that particular social formality.

"I'm not sure, Ken," he had answered. "With her, marriage just seems right."

I remembered what he had said, and I wondered why he would want to lie to her, what kind of marriage could be so deeply rooted in deception and still survive. She was straight--very straight--a young woman raised on an Iowa farm where weeds just got in the way of the corn crop, and chemicals were just a part of the fertilizer. All right, then, if he wanted her to be straight, in fact, loved her for it, he had no business lying to her about his past or continuing secretly the dope activities he knew she would disapprove of.

Maybe in the face of lies, of deceptions and the prospect of a life filled with such deceptions, he just got scared and ran. I could understand that all right. I had left a lot of things. However, I had never left a person holding a heart full of empty promises.

I came to the city square, an Iowa town square with its bandshell and flag pole serving as tributes to a life immortalized by Herbert Hoover and Meredith Wilson. In this case, though, the square served as a gathering place for the town's young. I threw my gear on an empty bench and sat down, looking at the evening traffic. At one corner were a few aging greasers in their hot, super fast cars. They were a vanishing breed. Hot cars had stepped aside for practical vans and hearses. The beer set was nearly gone. In their place were the shaggy, unkempt, drug-using freaks of Trans-Amerika.

I sat back and looked around the square. The small group of serious nodding faces around a blue van meant one thing--dealing. I smiled and felt comfortable in the company of drugs being sold and exchanged. I thought back to high school and when a small group of us would quickly do a number before classes. Things had certainly changed in town since then. I smiled and reached into my pocket for my stash and papers, looking up and seeing a patrol car drive by, I put them away again. Fort Dodge hadn't changed that much. The cops wouldn't be too cool about open smoking.

I left the bench to throw a Frisbee around with a group of freaks for awhile. Then I returned to my packs, threw them on my shoulder and once again started walking, alone, down the familiar alleys and paths toward the river. The night was a little chilly, and I stopped to put my jacket on. As I stood there in the dark, feeling the leather collar against my neck, I looked up to the stars. The night sky in Iowa didn't seem as awesome and grand as the starry displays in Montana or Wyoming. As I stood there looking up, hands in my pockets, my mind traveled back to what Denny had said that morning.

"I think you'd better get involved in something pretty soon, or you'll be in trouble."

"Maybe I am involved in something now," I thought. I remembered the afternoon with Mel. Maybe she needed me. I knew she needed answers to quite a few questions. Maybe I could be the one to answer some of them; maybe I could help her find herself amid the confusion and despair of a torn, shattered love.

I continued walking toward the river, thinking of Melody and Steve and a world of maybes and whys floating around about them, a world I was now somehow part of.

Finding a sheltered spot by a tree, where I could see the stars reflecting off the dark water of the river, I unrolled my bedroll and went to sleep.

REUNIONS IN SUMMERTIME

I tossed my packs on the sidewalk and sat down. "I was involved," I thought, "actually doing something to help someone else." I looked up at the sign above a nearby door. In bold hand-painted letters it read: "MIDAC (The Mid-Iowa Drug Abuse Council)." I leaned back on the pack feeling tired, a kind of emotional weariness that I had never felt before pressed down on me. I was trying to find Steve, trying to find some answers for Melody. In my own way, I was trying to pick up the pieces of her shattered life. The trail had brought me to Des Moines and this building.

All the while I was looking for leads, I had also been with Mel. Her calm self-confidence that most people saw in public would vanish quickly when we were alone. The tears would fall and the talks would stretch far into many nights. I reached deep into an unknown part of me to try to find a strength I could share with her. Her dreams were of blood and brutal death. She saw her impending murder constantly behind sleep-closed eyes. Her fears made her tremble when awake and scream silently in her sleep.

The one person she turned to, cried to, clung to as a refuge and comfort, was me. Her words of gratitude and prayers of hope were all directed toward a road freak who had always run from emotional commitments.

For the first time in my life, I was trying to accept someone's need for me to provide security in a world of insanity. As I lay awake at night, on her living room floor or in my bedroll by the river, I would feel afraid. How could I pretend to give advice or comfort when I had never known how to do the same for myself. I would lie there and convince myself that it would be best for both of us if I would just move on. I was a street freak, not a social worker, and I felt she needed more help than I could offer.

But the next day, I would be back, trying to make her smile, trying to make her forget the loneliness and despair caused by Steve's abandonment. The determination I would have to leave would vanish when I saw a candle of a smile break through and light the darkness of her gloom for a moment.

I sat on my packs on the Des Moines sidewalk before following up the next lead. I wanted to find Steve and the answers. At the same time, I was afraid. I had obviously taken a side in this thing now. My reasons for finding him were no longer concern for him. My reason was a growing affection for a blond-haired girl a hundred miles away. With my part in the drama already chosen, I felt I had betrayed an old friend who was apparently very much lost himself.

I reached into my pocket for some weed and papers. It was strange, but for the last week with Mel in Fort Dodge, I hadn't done much weed and no psychedelics. My mind simply wasn't able to handle deep, personal, drug-induced introspection and at the same time try desperately to relate to another human being's emotional needs.

I smiled and put the dope away, stood up with my gear and headed for the door.

Inside, I saw two girls behind the desk. They were young-looking, but their eyes and serious faces gave evidence to a worldliness that ignored age by years.

"How do?" I said, dropping my things on the floor and leaning on the desk.

"Hello, there. Can we help you?" said one, eyeing me and my packs.

"Yeah, uh, about a week ago, did you have a dude name Steve Butler crashing here?" I asked. "He may not be using that name. He's tall, good-looking, very dark hair, parted in the middle."

"Why do you want to know?" the second girl asked defensively. "Are you a cop or something?"

"What!" I exclaimed. "God no! Steve and I used to travel together. I was in Iowa, heard he was here and thought I'd look him up!"

"Hey, look at his pack," the first girl said. "Trans-Amerika, same as Steve's. He's probably cool."

"Thanks, lady," I said. "I take it he was here then. Is he still around?"

"No, he's gone. He and some chicks moved to a farm outside Ames about two, three days ago."

"Well, O.K.," I said, picking up my things. "Appreciate it." I raised a clenched fist in farewell. Feeling both weary and happy, I turned for the door. The trail was down to a few days old and still in Iowa, and I hoped it would be over in a few more days.

"Keep your screens clean, dude!" called one of the girls as I reached the door. I raised my hand without looking back and walked down the steps to the sidewalk.

The sun was going down as I headed for I-35 north to Ames. I wanted to see Mel before I slept that night. That kind of feeling was something I hadn't had for a long time.

That afternoon when she gave me a lift to the highway on my way to Des Moines, I had wanted to thank her for the time we'd spent together that week, but I couldn't. Instead, I reached over and kissed her on the forehead. She had drawn back, surprised, but squeezed my hand and smiled as I left the car.

I remembered that touch of her hand and the silent smile in her eyes as I held my thumb out for a ride. It was for those eyes and that smile that I was following Steve's trail to Ames.

The sky was dark and familiar constellations dotted the sky with light as I walked along a country road outside of Ames. A bad turn by my last ride and a lot of time on the freeway outside Des Moines had put me on a deserted gravel road in the dark at the north side of Ames. I was close to what the last couple of weeks had been about. I remembered the patrolman in Wisconsin and wondered where I'd be now if he hadn't had a weird memory for names and places. I smiled and looked up to the stars, feeling small beneath them all. I walked past a farm house and wondered if that was where Steve was living.

As I thought of Steve, I began to feel cold and afraid again. What would I say to him? How would I act? How would he act? What would he say to me? A car came by and I flagged it down.

"How do?" I said, throwing my gear inside and climbing in.

"Hello, son," said the driver, a middle-aged man. "Where are you going?"

"Into town, sir," I said. "Say, where do the college kids and freaks hang out?"

"Well, I don't know, son. I'll drop you off by the campus though. You'll find someone who knows. Are you trying to find drugs?" he asked in a non-committal voice.

"No," I said, raising my eyebrows in mild surprise at the casual question. Drugs were usually immediately damned to a burning hell by persons his age. I was curious why he was so casual about a subject I tried to avoid when traveling with his peers. "No drugs, man. I'm just looking for a dude in Ames."

"Too bad," he said, answering with a light smile. "If you'd have wanted to cop, I could have saved you some trouble. Here, try this, kid. It's the best in this part of the country." He took a small, thin number from the pocket of his white shirt and lit it. After taking a deep hit, he passed it to me.

"Far out, man!" I laughed and accepted the weed. I took a long toke almost finishing the thing and held the smoke deep inside my lungs as I passed it back to him. He reached inside his pocket for a jeweled roach clip and attached the rest of the joint. He took a hit, a small one, and passed it back to me.

My head was reeling from the first hit. The dope was great. I had done some great one or two hits hash, but never one-hit grass before. I took another long pull and collapsed in the seat. I watched the dash lights reflect off the jeweled clip, wondering if it was real.

"Pop it, son," said the man. "We're coming into town."

I ate the roach and the next few minutes lasted hours as I watched every crack in the sidewalk in Ames. He left me off and I staggered to a corner, completely wrecked. I looked for him, but he was gone, "Christ," I thought, "what dynamite weed. I wonder where he was from."

I picked up my gear, shook my head and started walking toward the nearest light. "Hey, man," I said, collaring a nearby freak. "I just hit town. Where's the best place to go to find a musician friend who lives in this town?"

"The Cave Inn, about four blocks that way," he said and pointed up the street. "Where you coming from?"

"Uh," I thought for a moment, my drugged mind trying to remember a city. "Oakland," I said. It was the first city in a series that came in mind.

"Good luck, man," he said, laughing, as I walked in the direction he was pointing.

My mind was slowly straightening itself out a little as I walked to the Cave Inn. A month ago, I had been in

California, walking on the beaches, panhandling and shoplifting in a dozen cities. I wasn't thinking about the future then. In fact, I rarely thought beyond the next ride or number. Now I was walking toward a restaurant in the heart of Amerika, feeling more afraid with every step. It had been quite a while since I'd seen Steve. He'd probably been through plenty himself, and I was afraid of how he might react to my reasons for looking for him.

The city seemed the same as a hundred or a thousand others. The sidewalks were as hard, and the lights were just as bright. As I walked, I remembered the other places, other sidewalks, other lights. The difference was that here, unlike other places, I had a reason for walking along the streets.

I slowed my pace when I thought of my reason. Her blue eyes and soft smile stayed with me all the time. I wanted those eyes to shine with joy and her smile to reflect hope, instead of the lonely, frightened darkness now clouding her face.

The Cave Inn was a combination bar and restaurant. Since I was twenty and the state drinking age then was 21, I couldn't go into the downstairs bar. As I climbed the stairs to the restaurant section, my head was still in a state of reeling numbness from the fantastic dope. I wouldn't know what to do with booze anyway. I was too stoned to be drunk. I smiled at the irony of the situation. Childhood Amerikan fantasies came to mind. "Who was that man?" "I don't know, but he just left me this great dope (or silver bullet)." I shook my head, trying to get clear before going inside.

I saw an empty booth and went to it, throwing my packs into one side and peeling off my jacket. It felt good to be free of the weight for awhile. I sat down and ordered a soft drink. The place was clean and roomy, a large juke box sat in a corner, but it wasn't loud enough to stop conversation. This place was like a hundred others, music to give a happy atmosphere, beer for those old enough to buy it, and plenty of tables to spread pizzas and hamburgers out. It was a place to talk to friends and make new ones before becoming lost in the world of darkness and loud music that the rock bars offered.

I stood up next to the booth with both my jacket and drink in my hands. I dropped my jacket over the back of the booth and looked around at the people. There were booths and tables occupied by couples deep in their private conversations and others occupied by laughing groups of beer-drinking, pizza-eating Iowa freaks. I looked, but I couldn't see Steve. If he was living in or around Ames, this would be the kind of place he would frequent.

I took a drink and sat down my glass. Wiping my lips, I headed for a table where two couples were sitting. The guys' hair was long, and their beards were shaggy. Both girls and guys were dressed in the patched denim uniforms of Trans-Amerika.

"How do, folks?" I said, feeling nervous and shaky because of the reason for being there and the dope I'd done earlier. "Do you people know a Steve Butler? Tall, good-looking dude with dark hair parted down the middle."

One guy looked at me, his eyes narrowing slightly as he made a slow mental inventory of my entire appearance. My dark blue shirt was open at the neck, revealing a string of beads partly hidden under my red scarf. My hands were both resting on the table, one wrist wrapped in a studded leather band, the other covered by my Indian bracelet. The belt holding up my faded jeans was braided leather, tied at my side and falling to fringed beaded ends hanging almost to my knees. My knife hung in its metal sheath from the belt. The man's eyes rested for a brief moment on the knife then moved up to meet my own nervous stare.

"No, I don't know him," he said in a slow, even voice. "Wouldn't tell you if I did, though. You're probably a cop."

"What the hell!" I started, raising my voice and drawing back. "Look, man, I'm just looking for a dude. Trying to find an old friend, and that's the second time today I've been called a cop. If you don't know him, and can't help me, fine. But just get off the cop shit."

I quickly turned around and headed for another table and other people. When I reached the nearest one, the girl sitting there said, "Forget it, man. That guy says you're a cop, and I'm not having any part of it."

I stood next to her table and looked at her. The rage I felt a moment earlier was gone. Instead, a feeling of impotence came over me. If these people could help me, they wouldn't because they thought I was a cop. I had been called a lot of things, by a lot of people, in earnest and in jest, in anger and fear, but I had never been denied help before because people thought I was a cop. I looked at the woman and raised my finger to begin pleading my case when I glanced at the booth behind her.

A guy sat in the booth staring at me, almost as if he knew me. I drew back in recognition. His long dark hair was sweeping over his back, wire-rimmed glasses shielded a pair of laughing eyes, and his pierced ear was hung with a roach clip earring. I smiled through my anger and dope-fogged mind.

"Karl," I said with laugh and sat down. "Remember me? Less than a month ago in Wisconsin? We went to Winona?"

He burst into a laugh and lowered his head a bit saying, "Jesus, man. I thought it was you. I'm sorry I didn't recognize you." He held out his hand, thumb high, to take mine. "Hey, Frank, you idiot, come here," he called to the first table and the guy I first talked to.

"You know this guy, Karl?" he said, throwing his thumb toward me and sitting down in the booth next to Karl.

"Oh, yeah, I do, Frank. I even gave him some of that acid you were dealing a few weeks ago," said Karl. "This clown's cool, so cut that cop talk and help him out if you can."

"I'm sorry," said Frank, "I really am. I guess I've just been jumpy lately. We've had a few busts here. There's quite a few narcs prowling around. Know what I mean?"

"Yeah, I do" I said, giving him my hand. "Don't worry about it. Do you know Steve? Or can you put me on to someone who does know him? He's supposed to be living on a farm around here with a couple of chicks."

"Yeah, I've met him, I think," he said. "If we mean the same dude, that chick owns the farm." He pointed to a woman standing by the door talking to a waitress. "Hey, Marla, come here," he shouted, getting her attention. He waved her over to the booth.

"Hi, Frank, Karl, what's happening?" she said. She was a tall, pretty girl wearing a blue work shirt tied around her midriff. She had a worn leather flyer's jacket thrown over her shoulder, and her hair was tied up in a blue scarf.

"Hi, Marla," said Frank. "What's that new dude's name living on your farm?"

"Steve," said Marla, motioning me to move over in the booth so she could sit down, otherwise though, she was ignoring me.

"Yeah, Steve," continued Frank. "Well, this dude here is looking for him." He pointed to me.

"Why do you want to find him?" she asked suspiciously.

"Well," I answered, "it's kind of a long story, but it's pretty important that I talk to him. I'm not going to hurt him or anything, so don't worry. Has he ever mentioned Kenny in Fort Dodge?"

"Yeah, he said he was busted with a guy named Ken there, about a year ago. Are you him?" she said.

I shook my head and asked her how she had met him.

"I just met him this week," she said. "I've been gone awhile. He met a friend of mine, Jean, at MIDAC in Des Moines, and they got it on real good. They decided to come live on the farm awhile. Look, I'm going back there now. Come with me, and explain it on the way."

I thanked Karl and Frank for their help and promised to see them soon. I put on my jacket and threw my gear on my back, starting out the door. Marla stopped me and looked at my pack.

"That's really a lot like Steve's. I guess you do know him. I haven't seen anybody else with one like that before."

She had a station wagon with the back seat taken out and replaced by a large mattress. I threw my gear inside, and she started driving toward the farm. I sat in the seat next to her, and for a few minutes neither of us said anything. I lay my head back, the effects of the dope had been pushed to the back of my mind during the last half hour. I was nervous, afraid. It had been awhile since I'd seen Steve, and I didn't know how I'd feel when we met.

"Why do you want to find Steve?" she said. "It's obviously more important than just looking up an old buddy, right?"

"That's for sure," I mumbled almost to myself. "Would you like to do a number while I explain it?" She shook her head, and I began to roll one.

"It's like this, Marla," I began. "Quite awhile ago, Steve got engaged to this chick in Fort Dodge." I took a long pull on the joint and passed it to her. I held the smoke deep and remembered Mel's face that day. It seemed so long ago now. "Anyway," I said, "they were supposed to be married this month, but about two months ago, he split for Denver where he was supposed to be working some sort of job. And his fiance hasn't heard from him since."

Marla shook her head slowly, steering the car with one hand and shaking ashes from the joint into the ash tray with the other. Her face was thoughtful for a moment, then she spoke, softly at first, then finishing with determination.

"Maybe he's not ready to marry her. Maybe she was really pushing him into it, and he had to split. If he doesn't want to get married, neither of you should try to force him!"

I took the number, now burned down to a roach, and clipped it. I felt a tension in the car as we drove along the gravel road toward the farm. I took two short tokes off the dope and handed it back to her in a vague effort to ease the strain.

"No," I said. "Nobody's trying to force him into anything. She just wants to know why. Like he left her with the invitations made, the rings to pay for, everything to get ready. Suddenly, he's gone. She just wants to know why. I don't think he should marry her either, not if he don't want to, but, Jesus, he does owe her at least a few answers."

"You know, Ken, I don't know this girl he was engaged to," said Marla, holding the clip in her hand, the fire gone from the number, "but I do know Jean, and I know she loves him. I don't want anything to hurt her."

"That's just it," I said. "Jean's got to know a few things too. She deserves to know why Steve left a chick after making a lot of promises to her without so much as a goodbye. It's not fair for Jean either, living with a guy about whom she knows nothing. Man, like I don't want to force anything on anybody, but for Christ's sake, everybody involved in this mess has got a right to know the score. That goes for Jean too, so if you care about her, please help me!"

"O.K. You're right," Marla snapped. "You're right. Jean's just been a good friend for quite awhile," she added, her tone suddenly softening. "She's been burned by a couple of guys before, and I don't want to see it happen again."

I looked at her and thought of her concern, a concern very close to mine. A friend of hers had been hurt, and she simply wanted to make sure it didn't happen again. Marla turned the car into the driveway of a small farm. "Here it is," she said as we got out of the car. "Sleazy Acres."

There was a large barn in need of a paint job, but otherwise looking pretty good. Flanking it were a couple of tool sheds and garages. The house was a typical, weatherbeaten Iowa farmhouse--the sort of plain, white frame thing where Aunty Em and Dorothy could have strolled in and called it home. There was a large yard surrounding the house. The grass was feshly mowed, and in the center of the yard was a big tree with several ropes dangling to the ground (purely recreational, I assumed, since the state took care of its own hangings).

"How many folks live here?" I asked in a light tone, designed to ease my own nervousness.

"Six, counting Steve now, and together we're able to pay the bills," she answered. "Steve's not working or anything yet, but Jean's got a little saved."

"Yeah," I mumbled. "I can really dig a scene like this." As we walked to the door, a girl came out to greet us. She was short with dark curly hair and round steel-rimmed glasses.

"Jean," said Marla, "This is Kenny, a friend of your old man. He's been looking for Steve for awhile. Where is he?"

"Hi, Kenny," she said in a bright tone, accepting a friendship I knew wouldn't be there in a few minutes. "Steve's gone for tonight. He'll be back sometime tomorrow. Come on in and do a bottle of wine with us."

I followed them both into the house, looking around at the walls and floors. Wondering how to go about telling this girl the truth, my mind automatically flashed back to Melody and then to Steve.

And in silence, I screamed at him. "Damn you, Steve! Damn your lying soul! How can you take two women who love you and use them like this? One's hurt a hundred miles from here, and to help her I'll probably have to hurt this one! Steve, how could you do this to any of us?!"

"Hey, dude, sit down," said Marla, motioning me to a chair. Her voice was softer than before, the tension between us was relaxing, and her eyes anxiously searched mine.

"Jean," I began, "how did you meet Steve?"

"Why do you want to know?" she answered looking up at me in my chair from her place on the floor, her tone simply curious.

"Well, it's not that I'm just nosy," I said in a shaking voice. "I'm looking for Steve because of some things he didn't take care of back home."

"What do you mean?" she asked. "He said he was just drifting when he came to Des Moines. He'd been living in Mexico since getting busted in Fort Dodge, but that was almost a year ago. Hey," she said, brightening in recognition, "you must be the dude he was living with then!"

"Yeah," I sighed, "that's me, Jean. But Steve's never lived in Mexico and he wasn't just drifting when he came to Des Moines; he was running scared!"

"What's going on?" she said, her voice taking on a worried tone, her eyes shot from me to Marla, then back to me. "Was he running from you, Ken?"

Marla got up and left the room. "I'll get the wine," she said, and I nodded.

"No, he wasn't running from me. Up until last month, he lived in Fort Dodge and worked as a shoe clerk." I leaned forward, and with each word spilling up from me like a nervous vomit, I poured out the whole story. When I finished, I sat back in the chair, my hand gripping the ornamented arm rests to keep from shaking.

Jean got up from the floor and walked to a dark, curtainless window. I saw her hands shaking as she absently fingered a tall potted marijuana plant by the window. Her hand left the plant and went to her eyes. She didn't cry, though; she just removed her glasses and cleaned them with the tail of her blue work shirt.

Then she turned to me, and in a slightly broken voice said, "What do you want now, Ken? Do you want me to give him up, send him back with you--to her? Is that it?" Her voice became louder and more determined with each word. "Well, I won't, I don't care what he's done. I love him, and I think we can make it! Who do you think you are coming here and demanding that he goes back? If he wanted her, he'd be there right now, but he's not! He's here with me!"

"Hold it, there lady," I said, breaking in and causing her to sit down. She lit a cigarette, her eyes flashing sparks at me. "I don't want him to come back with me," I said. "Christ, you're right! If he wanted her, he'd be there now. That's not what I'm here for. I'm just here to get a few answers, that's all! I think that girl in Fort Dodge deserves at least an explanation, and I came looking for him to get those answers."

"It's kind of like this," I continued. "Steve and I've been friends for a long time, and all the time I've been wandering around with no place to go or no one to go to, Steve's been in Fort Dodge. I mean, not just living in the town, but living there by choice. Shit, if he really wanted to be alone and moving, all he had to do is pick up his gear and split. That's just it; he didn't want to. He always told me that he wanted to get married and live a life that was comfortable."

"I used to laugh at him for falling into the Amerikan dream of a white picket fence and backyard barbecue. All the time, I was traveling and poking around here and there and nowhere, I knew in the back of my mind that Steve had his spot in life picked out and was probably happier than me. When I found out he'd given it all up or somehow lost it all, I went to find out why. Along that route, I met his girl and became very fond of her, so I decided to find out for both of us."

After finishing this speech, I collapsed back into the chair exhausted, thinking maybe I'd said too much about things that this girl knew nothing about. I looked up to find Marla holding a bottle of wine and handing it to me.

"Sorry it took me so long," she said with a wide grin.

"Coward," I answered, returning the grin and taking a deep pull from the wine.

Jean came over to the chair and took her turn at the wine. After handing the bottle back to Marla, she said, "I'm sorry I talked to you that way, Ken. I guess if I was in that girl's place, I'd be very thankful if a dude like you came along to help me out.

"I guess Steve and I have a lot of things to thrash out before we can ever really make it," she continued. "I wasn't really mad, just upset. I didn't want to believe that Steve would lie like that. He's coming back tomorrow, and I'll let you talk to him before I do, O.K.?" she said, her eyes wet with unshed tears.

"Ken," said Marla, breaking a silence of several minutes. "Do you have any of that weed left? We're out here."

"Sure," I said and smiled, feeling the tension break away like chips from a sculpture of a friendship. I rolled a couple of numbers and lit one, passing it to Jean.

The rest of the night was spent in the happy, smoking,

laughing, stoned party time of Trans-Amerika. The rest of
the residents of the "Sleazy Acres" farm had come home,
bringing more dope and wine. We got to know each other
amid the sounds of stereo and the smoke of dope. I slept well,
curled up in my bedroll in an attic room with the night air
blowing in on me from a nearby broken window.

The wind was a little colder and there was a touch of
moisture in the air as I woke. The sound of a car idling in the
driveway woke me, and I sat up quickly, shielding my eyes
from the brightness of the day. Looking out the broken
window, I saw Steve standing beside the car talking to the
driver. With a wave, he turned from the driver and walked
toward the house.

He seemed taller than I'd remembered. His hair was just
as dark as before, parted in the middle and falling in heavy
waves around his shoulders. He was wearing a leather vest
and a gold chain around his neck, hanging to his bare chest.
His jeans were worn and patched, but brightened by a few
embroidered designs. On his wrist was a black band studded
by silver stars, and he had his leather jacket thrown over his
shoulder.

As I was looking out the window, I felt my stomach
tighten, and I quickly looked to my wrist and my leather
band, and then to my jacket next to me on the floor, both
memories of what was once friendship.

Throwing my gear together, I hurriedly went down the
stairs, nervous about seeing the person responsible for the
roads I had traveled for the last few weeks.

"Ken's here!?" I heard him exclaim. "Where? When did
he get here?"

"Last night," I said, walking toward him.

"Kenny, it's you!" he said with a whoop of joy, throwing
his pack into the corner. I glanced at it, the large leather star
in the middle and above it the words "Trans-Amerika."

"How do, Steve," I said nervously. "You look good." I
held out my hand, thumb high, for the traditional handclasp.

We were alone in the living room. Marla, Jean and the
rest had noiselessly slipped off somewhere. We sat down on
the floor in front of the sofa, and Steve started talking in an
excited voice about how I'd gotten there, how I'd found him.
But I cut him short with a curt, nervous shake of my head.

"Steve," I said, "look, man, this isn't really a social

call.''

"Why, what is it?'' he answered, his dark eyes growing darker and the smile fading.

"I think you know, guy,'' I said slowly and softly, then rapidly continuing without giving him a chance to speak. "I've been looking for you since you got popped in Wisconsin, Steve. I've been to Fort Dodge, and I've seen Mel. Man, Steve,'' I said, my voice raising, "that girl is hurting!''

He quickly got up from the floor, and throwing his head back, shaking his hair behind him, he started walking across the room. He stopped at the window where a few dark clouds outside broke to let several rays of sunlight into the room. The potted marijuana plant was absorbing them and creating a leafy shadow on the bare wooden floor. He rested one hand on his hip, the other supporting him as he leaned against the wall. Bowing his head, his dark hair falling in front of and hiding his face, he stood silently for a moment before he spoke. With a slow, light shake of his head, he began.

"All right, you found me. So what?'' he said in a soft voice. "I can imagine what she's going through. Really I can. I've been hurting some myself. Jesus, I really didn't want to just run off like that. Really I didn't,'' he said, turning to face me, his back at the window and the sunlight reflecting off his dark hair. "I didn't want to just split; I just couldn't go through with it, that's all.''

"Fine,'' I said in a loud voice, slapping my palm with the back of my other hand. "Fine. Don't go through with it. If you don't want it, nobody's going to force you. But you better let that lady know why you don't want it.''

"How can I?'' he pleaded in a loud, choked voice. "I don't know why. It's a feeling in me, just a feeling. I can't sit down and analyze the whole thing. It just isn't that way at all.''

"Steve, she doesn't want you to analyze anything. She just has to know about those feelings, that's all,'' I said in a softer, less violent tone. "I mean, one day you tell her you're off to Colorado to work, and that's the last she sees of you. Did you even go to Colorado? None of us even know that much!''

"Yeah, I went to Colorado, and I got the job!'' he said. "I wasn't sure I wanted to go through with it even then, but I figured if I had work, and we could live in Colorado instead of Iowa, we could make it. Man, Ken, I couldn't live in Fort Dodge anymore. I couldn't, and I couldn't live there with a wife most of all.

"So I got the job in Colorado, hoping that we really could make it. I worked that mother-jumping job one day, and the next day, the foreman came in and said, "You, you and you--cut! We're overloaded." And he canned three of us just like that! Well, that tore it. I hung it all up right then and there. I just started moving after that and came to Des Moines a couple of weeks ago, met Jean and decided to try to make it here."

He sat back down on the floor next to the potted plant and began to absently stir the soil with a pencil. He continued softly, "Maybe I couldn't face her like that. Maybe I couldn't make her understand how I felt. Maybe that's why I never went back. I guess I was just afraid to face her!"

"I know, Steve," I said. "I really do. I can understand the whole thing, and you're doing right not getting trapped in a marriage you don't want. Still, Steve, you got a lot of loose ends to tie up back there before you can try anything here. What about the lies you told these people here? Mexico, and no telling what else. What's wrong with you, anyway? You can't just pretend with people who love you."

"I shouldn't, Ken, I know I shouldn't," he said. "But I did, I do and I can't undo it now. What can I tell Melody? Do I say I just stopped loving her? It's not that cold, not at all. Maybe I still love her, but I can't marry her. I know I could never be the kind of husband she wants."

"Look, man," I said in an almost harsh voice, "I don't care what you say to her as long as you try to make her understand why! Let her know where she stands now! She's got to know that you won't come popping into her life like a bad dream. Cut her loose, man. Tie up those ends, and let her have a life without you! I can't do anything for her along those lines. Only you can, and I want you to go back to Fort Dodge and take care of it. And I'm not leaving here until you do!"

Leaning toward him and raising my finger, I spoke in a low, threatening voice. "I didn't come to Iowa for any hassles, Steve. But the lady's been hurt enough, and if you don't go back and explain things to her, god help me, I'll break your goddamned neck!'' I closed my fist quickly because my finger began to shake violently with my anger.

"Hey, man," Steve said quickly and loudly. "Cool it! I know you're right, and I'll talk to her! You don't have to make threats. Christ, we've been through too much shit together to let this break up our friendship! I was wrong. I knew it then, and I know it now. I probably would have gone back on my own sooner or later anyway!''

"You're right," I said, my anger subsiding. "I'm sorry. When do you think you're going back?

"All right--next Tuesday. Jean will have the car back," he said. "She'll give me a lift up there, hang out someplace while I see Melody, and we'll come back afterwards. O.K.? Is that good enough for you?''

"Yeah, fine," I said. "I just want to be sure. Well, Steve," I said, standing and walking to the window, bright with sunlight, the clouds all gone by then. "I guess I got done with what I came to Iowa for. I'll go back to Fort Dodge and tell Melody.''

"Hey, man," Steve said. "Why don't you hang around here for awhile? The people are beautiful, and I'm sure they'll be glad to have you. I know I'd like you to move in here. It could be like before. We had some good times, man...''

"No thanks, Steve," I said quietly as I looked at him on the floor. "I don't want to stay in Iowa. I just came to find you, that's all. Could someone here give me a lift into town? I'd better get going.''

"Sure," he said, getting up and taking my hand in both of his. "Marla's got to go in anyway. She's got to be at work by three. I don't know what I would have done if you hadn't shown up. I do thank you, Ken, and I'm sorry you had to find me like this.''

"Yeah, well," I muttered. "It's cool. Hang in there, man. I'll be seeing you.''

I went up to the attic and rolled my bedroll into shape again, tied my jacket to it and went downstairs again where Marla was waiting. I didn't see Steve when we went to the car. I didn't feel bad not seeing him. Just empty.

It was done, It seemed so long ago since I'd been cooling my feet in that stream, and it seemed somehow longer since I'd seen Mel, and I wanted very much to see her again before

I left Iowa.

The large, white house sat at the end of the block, its windows open to let the summer breezes enter. I could see the navy blue Corvair parked out front. I walked slowly, thinking of the past weeks. A coincidence by a Wisconsin stream had led to more coincidences and now to the door of a white house in Fort Dodge.

I remembered wondering what had happened, being afraid for Steve. That fear had changed to an affection for the blond-haired girl of his past. Steve was all right, living with half a dozen good people on a farm, and my fears for him were gone.

But the feelings I had for Mel weren't gone, and my stomach was clenched in a tight knot as I knocked at the door. It had only been about two days since I'd last seen her, but it seemed much, much longer. I wanted to see her very much, but at the same time, the reason I'd come to Iowa was gone, and it was time for me to be gone too.

I stood on the step with my packs at my feet, nervously fingering the belt on the bedroll, much the same as a man might absently pat a dog.

"Kenny? My God, it is you! I just knew it was, I knew it!" Mel opened the door, her blue eyes shining and her hair pulled back behind her neck. "Come on in," she said excitedly. "I'll get you something to drink. It's a hot day, and you look all sweaty."

I left my gear on the step and went inside. Sitting on the floor in front of the sofa, I watched her as she brought me a Pepsi in a large glass. I took it without looking into her eyes. We both knew why I was here, but neither knew quite how to begin.

"You found him, didn't you, Ken?" she asked quickly, breaking the momentary silence. She sat straight in front of me, not trying to avoid my eyes or shield herself in any way from my words.

"Yeah, Mel," I answered. "I found him alright. He lives on a farm near Ames."

"And...?" she asked, inviting more, demanding that I finish.

With my hands trembling slightly, I told her what had happened during the past few days.

When I finished, she looked at me with eyes slowly filling

with tears. "He's coming Tuesday, fine." she said. "But I don't know what to say to him. I'm afraid to see him. I can't see him now, not after everything that's happened!" Her voice broke and became a choking sob. "I don't ever want to see him. I don't care anymore. If he's happy, he's happy, great! But I don't want to know!"

I turned my face, not wanting to see her tears. "Look, Mel, he's going to come here Tuesday, and you had better ask him any questions you have."

"What about you, Kenny?" she asked in a rasping voice. "Where are you going to be?"

I shrugged my shoulders, still avoiding her tear-streaked face. "I did what I came here to do. I guess I'll go look at a mountain someplace."

"No! Goddamn it, no!" she said loudly. "I won't see him unless you're here! I can't. Don't you understand, you can't leave now? Wait until after Tuesday. Please!" she said, clutching my arm.

"All right, I will," I answered, looking into her eyes. "What day's today?"

She ran her sleeve across the wet eyes, smearing the moist tears across her face. "It's Friday. That's only four days."

"Ail right. I'll be here Tuesday. He didn't say what time he'd be here so I'll show up early in the morning, O.K.?" I said.

"O.K. Where are you going until then?" she asked, her voice returning almost to normal.

"I'm not sure," I answered gruffly. "Too much has happened. I've gotten too close to you too soon, and I've got to go someplace to think. Maybe I should never have gotten mixed up in this whole mess. Maybe I've done more damage than good. I don't know anymore. I guess no one does," I added, almost to myself.

"Well, I know, Ken! Believe me, I do," she said, holding my hand, her voice sincere and kind. "You've helped me a lot. I don't know what I'd have done without you. Sometimes, I just feel like running and running and never stopping until I die. When you're around, I don't feel like that.

"You've been good to me, Ken. No one asked you to make my troubles your own. No one asked you to go looking for Steve because I had to see him. No one asked you to do any of it, but you did. You saw someone who needed help, and you tried to help her without asking anything for it.

"I can't even tell you how much I owe you. I wanted to die, God knows how many times I wanted to go out and do it, but you stayed with me, talking to me, helping me until I didn't feel like that anymore. Maybe I owe you my life. I don't know, but I owe you plenty. You say you've gotten close to me, well, I've become close to you, too. So don't think you've done bad."

"Fine, I won't," I said, standing up. "But as Gallahad, I've never quite made it. Don't thank me if you feel better now than before. Thank yourself. You did it, not me."

I went out the door to where my gear was waiting and threw the packs on my back. Turning with my eyes stinging full of unused tears, I said, "I'll be back Tuesday, Mel. Be awake. Bye for now!"

The next few days were spent laying around Fort Dodge. My spot by the river became a kind of late-night refuge. My head was lost in the dope-fogged numbness of marijuana the whole time. If not at the river, on the floor of some friends' pad amid the parties designed to block painful memories and thoughts by dope, booze and chemicals. Through the many moments, countless aching seconds and endless time of those few days, the images of blue eyes, laughing, filling with tears, sparkling with love, came flashing through to me, breaking past any barriers I tried to set up.

Monday night, I was sitting on the flag pole base at the city square. My mind was staggering in its dope-induced haze as I looked up to "Old Gory" proudly flying above the head of one, lone Trans-Amerikan freak. I was smoking a joint, oblivious to the possibility of Amerikan police invading my private sanctuary.

Tomorrow was the day, and by tomorrow night, I hoped to be out of Iowa and away from all the carnage left here by shattered bits and pieces of hearts.

"Kenny!! Hey, Ken!" I heard someone calling me, and I saw a familiar-looking stationwagon pull up.

"What the...!" I gasped, running toward the machine. Steve and Jean jumped out.

"Hi, guy!" I said. "Uh, what are you doing here? Like you're not supposed to show 'til tomorrow."

"I know," said Steve, "but Marla loaned us her car

today. Jean's car is still in the shop. Hey, man, I want to thank you for what you've done. Jean and I will be fine. She knows me a lot better now, thanks to you. I guess I know myself better too. You did all right, brother!''

''Yeah, sure,'' I mumbled through the fog inside my head. ''Mel. What about Mel? Has he been there?'' I thought.

''You seen Mel yet?'' I asked, fearing the answer.

''Oh, yeah, I just left her. Jean waited by the music store with the car.'' He smiled lightly. ''Funny, you didn't see her; it's only a block away.''

''How is Mel? She taking it all right?'' I asked in a trembling voice. My mind was slowly escaping the fog.

''Fine. She just wanted to give me back some stuff I left there, that's all. She wasn't as messed up as you said, Ken. You must have calmed her down pretty well. She accepted the whole thing. No questions or hassles, nothing, man.

''Hey, man,'' he continued. ''Can you spare a few numbers for the trip back? We left our stash at home.''

''Huh? Yeah, O.K., here,'' I muttered, tossing him the last of a lid in my pocket.

My brain was screaming at me, ''MEL! How is he?! She couldn't have been that calm, no way!''

''Hey, I gotta' split,'' I said. ''So long, Steve. Have a happy, you two!'' I started toward the street.

''Hey, dude!'' Steve called after me. ''When you coming to the farm?''

I didn't answer him because by that time, I had ducked down an alley and was running toward Mel's house. My brain running wild toward a place I should have been tonight. ''One day early, and I wasn't there,'' I thought, running faster, my feet beating a rhythm of failure along the pavement.

Stopping on the step for a brief moment to catch my breath, I saw her car and a light on inside the house. I opened the door and walked in abruptly.

She was sitting at the kitchen table, her head buried in her arms. I could hear no sound, but I knew from the movement of her shoulders that she was crying. She wore a pair of faded jeans, a bright yellow shirt, her hair in tangles around her folded arms.

I walked behind her and slowly, silently began to

massage her neck. She stopped crying, and for several minutes I just stood there calming her tense, tight nerves until she said in a cracked, broken voice, "He came, Kenny. He came, and you weren't here."

"I know, baby," I said. "I just saw him and came as quick as I could. I'm sorry."

My hands stopped moving on her neck as she got up and went into the living room without saying a word to me. Just as silently, I followed her. She sat down on the floor next to a long, flower print dress and idly picked it up with one hand.

"He gave this to me," she said softly to no one in particular. "He always wanted me to wear it." She let it drop again into a crumpled heap on the floor. She turned to me, and said in a voice that was nearly a whisper, "I wanted to give it back, but he wouldn't take it."

"Where were you, Kenny? I wanted to talk to you today, and I couldn't find you." Her lower lip trembled and the back of her hand went up to rub her eyes. Her entire face was red with tear streaks making damp lines down her cheeks.

"I didn't know what to say. There wasn't anything worth asking," she continued, tears breaking through the composure. "I didn't cry, though, Kenny. Really, I didn't. I wasn't going to let him see me crying over him. I just gave him the clothes and things he left here and let him go."

At that, she broke into a sob and leaned toward me. I caught her in my arms, resting her head on my shoulder, her tears dampening my filthy work shirt.

"Where were you, Kenny?" she sobbed once. But I couldn't answer her, the tears were choking my voice. For over an hour, we sat there, saying nothing as my hand rubbed her neck.

Later, I sat her up in front of me, took off my red scarf and dried her eyes. "Are you all right?" I asked.

She managed a small smile and shook her head. "I'm fine now, Kenny. Thank you."

I just smiled and put my scarf back on.

"He really did love me once," she said. "I know it. I guess I'll never really know what went wrong, will I?"

I shook my head, speaking in a soft tone, "I don't think any of us will--least of all, him."

She answered silently with her eyes, then went back to the dress on the floor. With her back to me, she asked, "Are you planning to leave, Ken?''

"Yeah," I answered, "this Iowa business is done for me. I'll get my packs and be gone in the morning."

"Will you get rid of this for me, please? I don't want it anymore," she said, handing me the dress without turning around.

I took it without a word and moved toward the door. She stopped me before I got there and put her arms around my neck. She reached up and kissed me, softly, gently, her lips tasting of salty tears. "That's to thank you," she said. My own eyes began to sting with tears, and my voice failed. I just smiled and walked out the door, clutching the dress in my sweaty hands.

I walked slowly along the streets, memories racing through me, visions of love playing patterns in my mind. I felt a tear crawl down my cheek, and I quickly-brushed it away. Remembering the dress, I stopped at a Goodwill box and stuffed it in. Looking up to the Iowa night sky, I stopped for a second, reached inside myself for the tears I vowed I would never spill on the streets of an Amerikan city and found they wouldn't come. Silently, with tears floating inside me, I stared at the Iowa sky.

PART IV

CALIFORNIA HIGHWAY

**"And through the mists,
wandering ever onward
in the motions of moisture,
the dampness of air
grown cold in the night..."**
                    Lyftogt

WESTERN SKIES

Fort Dodge was forty miles east of me as I walked along the dusty edge of Highway 20. I walked slowly with all the time in the world resting on my hands. The cornfields were endless jungles of green leaves, and the horizon was a flat green carpet blending with the blue summer sky.

I was alone again, and the way I figured it, I should be. How often had I pointed out to people that my section of Trans-Amerika just belonged to me? It wasn't big enough to share or stable enough for anyone to hang on to or love. Why, then, did I feel so alone? With a million people I had never met, waiting for me in a million places I had never seen; why did I feel like the only person alive at this moment?

Her eyes a soft blue, filled with tears, tore at my memories. Now we were both free from the responsibilities of love and friendship. Free to find whatever something or someone along our separate highways. I looked again at the flat, fertile, summertime landscape of Iowa and knew that I had to seek shelter among the rugged rocks and trees of a Western mountain range. Things were growing here. In less than a month, the fruits of a summer's growing would be harvested and stored for the winter. I wasn't a part of that harvest, and I knew I'd better leave before I forgot who I was and what I was.

I hadn't felt this alone since I'd laid my head on a beach at Big Sur a long time ago. Like so many things in so many places, I had left that beach and those people to find someplace and someone else to leave. Maybe it was time to go back now, to give up and lay back under a mountain flag. Forget the world outside the sun-sprinkled glade and rest forever amid the towering, god-like trees.

A blue van was slowly driving toward me as I walked backwards, thumb up, along the road. My thumb was up in hope. The van, an old Ford, pulled over, and I climbed in its side door. The driver was a short young man with large friendly eyes and a bright smile, capped by a twirling mustache. Next to him sat a large girl, who seemed plump in a happy, healthy way. Her dark eyes flashed light from beyond their darkness, and her darker hair fell in long curls to the center of her back. In the back, on a makeshift sofa, sat a smiling girl with light brown hair falling in smooth softness to her shoulders.

"Well, how do, folks?" I sighed in a tired voice as I sat on my packs against the wall of the van.

"Hello," said the girl across from me in the back of the van. "Where are you going?"

I felt so tired inside that conversation seemed impossible, so I just pointed west.

"How far?" she insisted, pointing west, almost forcing me into conversation. She wasn't demanding an answer, just trying to draw me into a harmless talk.

I grinned at her, and her light eyes danced in response. "Until I run out of land, I guess," I said in a brighter tone. "Where are you people from?"

"New Jersey," said the driver. "I'm Jay. That's Madilyn," he said, pointing to the dark-haired girl next to him, "and that's Chris back there." We exchanged smiles all around, soft, comfortable smiles as if they'd come over a thousand miles to give me a lift in the midday Iowa sun because they knew I was here waiting.

"Hi, I'm Kenny. Thanks a lot, group. I appreciate the lift. Where are you going that brings you to the wilds of Iowa?"

"School starts pretty soon," said Chris. "We just quit our jobs a little early and decided to travel before going back to books, tests and things."

"Yeah, that's cool," I answered. "It's a good land, good to see."

"What about you? asked Madilyn. "Do you live here in

Iowa or just passing through?''

''I went to high school in Fort Dodge,'' I said. ''Been on the move more or less ever since then. I got involved in some garbage here the last couple of weeks, but it's done now, and I'm leaving.''

''What kind of garbage.'' asked Chris. I looked at her and Madilyn, both happily, curiously involved in a conversation with a stranger. I didn't know how to explain the last few weeks to anyone. I wasn't quite ready to talk to anyone about it just yet.

''I tried my hand at being Galahad. But I found out that we knights in shining armor don't get paid by the dragons or the fair damsel.'' I must have sounded serious because their faces suddenly became sad. ''Hey, people, that was a joke!'' I said and forced a laugh that turned real, and in a minute we were all laughing at my joke about something they knew nothing about.

When we stopped laughing, Chris turned to me and said, ''What happened wasn't funny, was it?'' Then, seeing the look in my eyes, she added quickly, ''I'm sorry. I get too nosey sometimes.''

''It's O.K., really,'' I answered. ''You're right, but it's done now.''

Jay drove on silently as the rest of us exchanged tales about each other. Between the laughter and serious talks, we got to know each other. What Jay didn't say about himself, the girls filled in.

They were all well along in school and looking forward to finishing. Jay had saved a long time for the van, and all had looked forward to their vacation all summer. In a way, Jay and Chris were a couple, but not in a permanent sense. They were making the trip together because they had grown very close during the summer, both working in some place. After they got back, East, they would each probably go separate ways. Madilyn was a close mutual friend, and they wanted to finish this summer together.

After a few hours of driving and conversation, we crossed the South Dakota border.

''Well, so much for Iowa,'' I said as Jay slowed down for a small town roadside park.

''How about stopping here for supper, folks?'' he said.

''Hey, man,'' I answered, ''I know this town! Lived here

about a dozen years ago. Go in, and I'll show you a real nice little park--a lot better than a rest stop--it's only a couple of miles."

"Why not?" said Chris happily. "We've got time!"

"Great," Jay answered, not at all put off by the suggestion. "Let's have a few directions back there, partner."

Laughing and smiling, we rolled into the city park of Elk Point, S.D. It was a town of fewer than five hundred people, a friendly burg with clean streets and a pretty, well-kept park. I had gone to third grade here, and the homecoming was strange, and in a way, thrilling.

Before breaking out any food, Jay produced a happy freak's best friend--a Frisbee. "Just want to stretch my legs a little," he laughed, and a moment later we had a fine four-way game going.

"Do you know anybody in this town anymore?" asked Madilyn as she threw me the Frisbee.

"Not really. It's been quite awhile," I answered, spinning the disc to Chris. As we played on the soft grass, a feeling of warmth and friendship that had sprouted when I first met these people blossomed into a small, loving flower. I wanted to thank them for showing up when they did. I had about four dollars to my name, so there was no way I could show my gratitude with money. I knew we'd share my dope anyway, so it left me with few choices. "What kind of meal you planning?" I asked between throws.

"Just soup and sandwiches. We've got a portable stove in the van," said Chris.

"Far out," I said. "Hey, group, spin me out for a bit, will you? I want to check something out." I hadn't been forced to prowl the sacred aisles of a supermarket for food in the last few weeks, but now seemed a good time to get back in shape.

I walked into the small Safeway store. Just as I had hoped--it was crowded with evening shoppers. "Don't burn the people, but rip off the stores," I muttered as I picked up a large cantalope and began tossing if from hand to hand. The first rule in shoplifting is: "Keep your hands in sight and moving."

When I got back to the park, Chris and Jay were setting up the stove and Madilyn was buttering bread. "How do, folks?" I said, skipping into the park, still tossing my cantalope (which, incidently, I had paid for).

"Hi, Ken. Did you find what you were after?" asked Chris.

"Don't know a soul here anymore," I answered. "But I had thought I'd help with dinner. Do you like fruit?" and I tossed the cantalope to Jay. From under my shirt, I produced several cans of tuna, beans and some packaged meats. "I hope these will help out in the provisions department," I added.

Madilyn's eyes widened, and then she grinned. "You're a thief! You stole these, didn't you?"

I drew back in the classic pose of shock, my arm thrown in front of my face. "Madame, you wrong me greatly!" I said. "I merely liberated them." In a moment we were all laughing and giggling like a collection of fools at a jester's convention.

That evening's meal was one of the finest of my life. A meal is made up of food and love. What is lacking in food can be more than compensated by love, but if the love is missing, filet mignon is tasteless.

We drove late into the Dakota night after cleaning up from the supper and leaving the little park. With Jay and Chris asleep in the back, Madilyn and I talked along the miles of dimly lit road. None of them had ever been west before, and I inadvertantly became a guide. With the moon and stars making a million patterns across the darkness of night, I talked of the land. Somehow, the subject turned to the Indians, and for hours I talked of the beautiful, fierce tribes of the Sioux Nation, most of all the Oglala and their leader, Crazy Horse.

We would periodically break the conversation with an unaccompanied raspy song of traveling. Our two-person repertoire ranged from Woody Guthrie to Jim Morrison, from Pete Seeger to Ron Eliot. Our laughter brightened the darkness. We made up in enthusiasm for the lack of tone and harmony.

Early in the morning, our eyes too heavy to keep open any longer, we found a rest stop and pulled over to sleep. Jay and Chris made room for Madilyn in the back of the van. I took my gear and curled up under a nearby tree. Through its leaves, I could see the sky of the Dakota night, the sky that seemed larger here, and I knew it would grow even more as we went further west. I lay there, my hands behind my head, thinking of stars and skies.

Trans-Amerika became too beautiful to ever leave on nights like these. Friendships that I could never have in any other life became real here, things I could never see came my way every day. For the night, I forgot about the loneliness of the morning and the pain of a month of yesterdays. I slept well, deep, beneath the tree by a South Dakota highway.

In the morning the rays of the sun woke me to a chilly dawn. I looked at the van, its people not stirring yet, and I smiled to myself, a warm smile breaking the chill of the dew that covered my bedroll. I threw my jacket over my face and slept some more. The next sound was Jay's voice waking me gently to the late-morning breakfast.

Driving again, we talked of the land.

"What's good up ahead, Kén?"

"Well, we went through most of the dull parts last night. Pretty soon there's the Bad Lands and then the Black Hills," I answered.

We drove on, looking forward to mountains and trees, the beauty of a land rich in history and legends. With Chris picking out light tunes on a guitar, I talked of the Bad Lands and the Black Hills. I had never had a bad experience in South Dakota. The mountains always seemed teeming with friendly, helpful people.

I had been given the beads around my neck in South Dakota. I had partied on Mount Rushmore by a small dam with a bunch of freaks from Rapid City, ending with a freezing midnight swim. I glanced down at my foot as I spoke and remembered a party in the Bad Lands several months earlier.

A small group of us had helped a stranger package several keys of weed and were given a couple of lids for our efforts. Later in the day, stoned on weed and tripping on acid, we had gone running around the hills. In my stoned mind, I had forgotten how far I could jump and tried to leap across a large chasm. I had fallen maybe twenty feet and broken my foot. My friends hauled me up with ropes, and for the rest of the night I sat with it swelling and hurting in front of the campfire. The next morning, I had taken the scarf from my neck and tightly bound the foot. I pulled on my boot as a makeshift cast and didn't take if off for more than a week.

The foot had healed, but I walked a little weird because it healed crooked. But for the most part, my do-it-yourself doctoring had worked out quite well.

I finished my South Dakota stories with a laugh that everyone shared.

"Kenny," said Jay, "How do you live, just moving around like you do? I mean, don't you ever need money? How do you make it?"

I generally shrugged off that question. But these people had become more than just a ride. I didn't know how to explain my feelings to them or even myself, for that matter. I hoped my answer to Jay's simple question said what I felt.

"I make it, Jay," I said, looking at each of them, "because of the generosity of beautiful people like you."

To call someone beautiful in Trans-Amerika meant more than a physical appearance. And I could tell by Chris's smile that she understood.

That afternoon, we rolled into the Bad Lands of South Dakota. The Bad Lands were made up of mountains of eroded clay and prairies topped with grasses not found anywhere else. The clay mountains weren't soft and comfortable like the Black Hills or as grand and challenging like the Rockies. But they had a beauty, a kind of rugged sense of forever timelessness that made them unforgettable.

Leaving the van, we began to walk. Chris knew a little about botany, and she was extremely interested and excited about the many different kinds of plant and flowers. She would stop and bend over a small flower, gently pushing the grasses away from it. Like a delicate Madonna of nature, admiring her young, she would examine its color, its fragrance, with glowing eyes and a soft smile. I knelt next to her as she examined a small yellow flower and felt almost timid, like a man looking at someone else's baby, afraid to touch it, lest it be hurt, but wanting its mother to know that I too recognized its loveliness.

"Here, Ken," she said, plucking the flower. "You're both a part of this land." And she put the flower into the knot of my scarf.

I couldn't think of anything to say. The gesture was small, but like my answer earlier, it was meant to be much more. "Hey, Chris, careful. It's a bust to pick flowers here," I said in a small, light whisper. "But thanks, really, thanks a lot."

Sne smiled at me, her eyes shining, almost sparkling, and we walked to where Madilyn and Jay were standing.

"Hey, Ken," said Jay, pointing far up into the heights of a clay mountain, to a small ladder. "Look, I bet you could see for hundreds of miles from there. Let's climb it."

I looked up to the peak, dark clouds floating about the sky above it. "Well, it'll take awhile, but fine with me. How about you two?" I said, turning to Chris and Madilyn.

"No thanks, fellas," said Chris. "I'm no mountain climber."

"I'm not exactly Sir Edmund Hillary, either," I answered. "Come on."

But they both declined, and Jay and I found ourselves climbing alone. Climbing a big pile of dirt is a lot different than climbing rocks. No hand holds stay put, and no foot rests can be trusted. After an hour or so, we neared our destination. We were on a small ledge just below the ladder leading to the summit. We shook hands in mutual thanks and looked down to where Chris and Madilyn stood waving. Jay returned the wave, then drew his hand back quickly. "Do you feel what I feel?" he asked.

I felt it all right, coming down faster now--rain!

"Oh, no,!" I said. "Quick to the top, man!" and we both scrambled up the decrepit, rickety ladder to the summit.

I looked up at a large thunder cloud above us, the rain coming in torrents now. Jay was next to me, his head thrown back in laughter as he peeled off his shirt.

"Look at that!" he shouted. "We're standing above the whole world!" He laughed loud and long, throwing his arms out to embrace the universe, the rain splashing on his bare chest.

I began to laugh, and together we shared the mastery of the galaxy amid an almost blinding rain.

"Hey, man!" I shouted above the storm. "This clay mountain is now a huge pile of mud. Be prepared to live here, 'cause we can't climb down now!" With that, our laughter grew, and we both sat down in the mud, dangling our legs over the side, waving to the girls down below. They waved back, calling for us to come down.

"We can't!" I yelled. But they couldn't hear a word.

"Look at that slope," said Jay, his hair plastered to his face by the rain and his eyes laughing. "It was too steep to climb up, remember?''

"Yeah," I grinned and shook my head, scattering water all around me to mix with the torrents from the sky. "So what?"

"Can you ski?" he shouted with a large smile.

"You're kidding!" I said in surprise, getting his meaning. "Hey, dude, that's a long way down."

"Come on," he shouted. "I don't ski either!" He ran toward the slope.

In a second, we were both sking down a mud slope in the middle of a rainstorm. Arms flailing, voices high in laughter and screams, we slid. I looked at Jay and saw his feet fly out from under him, and with a yelp of surprise, he finished his slide on his New Jersey background.

I broke into a laugh at seeing Jay blaze a trail down the mountain with the seat of his pants. No sooner had I begun to laugh than my foot hit a piece of dirt, and I pitched forward. Sliding on my chest and stomach, I tried to turn around and imitate Jay, but just succeeded in causing myself to roll.

I hit bottom and a small clump of bushes at the same time. Jay slid safely into an upgrade to the left of me. I untangled myself from the twigs and thorns and with a laughing voice called out to Jay, who was soaked with rain and splattered with mud. "Hey there, fella', neither one of us can ski!"

Chris and Madilyn came running toward us, obviously to see if we were injured, but stopped short. They looked at us; I with my shirt in tatters and covered with mud, and Jay, bare-chested and caked in mud. We looked ridiculous, and they began to laugh; laughter then rang out of four people in a rainstorm.

"Ken!" said Jay. "I left my shirt up there!"

"O.K. Let's go back after it!" I laughed.

"Come on, both of you," said Madilyn like a disgruntled mother reprimanding two mischievous children. "Let's find a place for you to clean up!"

We traveled through most of Wyoming during the next two days. Acting as a guide, I told them of the towns in the area, most of which should be avoided. Sheridan, with its hostile police, and Gillete, with its hostile populace. Trans-Amerika wasn't particularly loved in the hard of Amerikan Cowboy country.

Perhaps we were hated because we resembled the long-haired, nomadic, beaded Indians more than the gun-toting, swaggering, tamers of the frontier. It was a heritage thing--their fathers and grandfathers had fought to make this land safe for Amerika. Could they do less against this latest breed of tribesmen?

We stopped at the top of the Big Horn mountains to look for a dent I had put into them quite awhile earlier with a friend's Ford. Going down the mountains, awed by the splendor and majesty of the peaks, Chris opened the skylight on the van. We stood up in the van with out torsos outside the top. Her head thrown back and long hair streaming in the wind, she laughed in silent joy. I stood next to her, my heart beating quickly, forgetting any pain, ignoring any sorrow, I felt I would burst with happiness as we drove through the grand monuments of nature.

As we stood there with the cool wind blowing our hair into the sky and whipping around our faces, Chris moved over to me. Arms wrapped around each others necks and hair mingling in the breeze, we shared the beauty of the afternoon.

By evening, we'd set up camp in Yellowstone National Park. I had come to nearly despise Yellowstone during my last few visits there. The hours of waiting to get in, the ugly checkerboard marked campsites, and the thousands of tourists visiting nature while carrying suburbia with them in their trailers. The beauty of the geysers was almost spoiled by a collection of beer cans and gum wrappers floating in the steaming water. Old Faceful erupted right on time as usual and was surrounded by cameras, parking lots, and souvenir shops.

The park, with its hot springs, geysers and occasional animals, had become the highest status symbol for suburbanite campers. The beautiful lands, majestic mountains and clean, cold lakes meant nothing. A million other parks had those things, but they weren't bristling with tourist gift shops or boasting camping facilities that could accomodate all the appliances contained in the modern camper.

The poor couldn't come to Yellowstone. The entrance fees, the camping fees, the washroom fees and the constant temptation of the shops, restaurants and souvenir stands added up. They added up to a point where the one-car, one-tent family became lost in the mire and muck of the same financial, social jungle they left behind in the city. It had become simply a place for the rich to flaunt their wealth and bastardize a once-beautiful site.

Above most trailers stood a T.V. antenna, and at night the peace and quiet of the forest would be broken by the reruns of ''Bonanza.''

But my New Jersey friends had never seen Yellowstone, and despite the fact that it now belonged to the gods of Madison Avenue, the first look is still nearly impressive.

We found a place to camp just as the sun was going down. I left the three to set up the campsite and went off in search of firewood. Using a small saw and hatchet of Jay's, I spent the next couple of hours sawing large tree limbs off dead trees and chopping them into usable portions.

I went back to the camp with enough wood to start a fire, then quickly returned to the forest to cut more. I cut much more than we needed. It wasn't because I enjoyed the work--in fact, my hands had sprouted a half dozen painful blisters--but I just felt like being alone among the trees and bushes. The sky was dark and brilliantly lit by more stars than I could count. I took the last of the wood back, returned the tools and made some excuse to leave, to hurry back to the forest.

Not far from where the van was parked was a large lake. I just walked through the forest until it stopped at a rocky shore. I squatted on the edge of the dark, cold-looking water and idly skipped rocks across, listening to the splashes I couldn't see. I was getting colder as the night deepened. I wished I had on more than just a shirt, but I didn't feel like returning for my jacket. I didn't want to see people or metal cars or plastic domed tents or T.V. antennas or forty-foot trailers. I didn't want to hear little children whine as they tugged at their mothers' sleeve, ''There's nothing to do!'' I didn't want to hear the news of the world from either radio or T.V. or hear some disgruntled wife complain to her husband, ''Henry, it's cold. Won't you please get that heater going?''

At the moment, all I wanted was the solitude of a dark night and the shore of an even darker lake. I lay back on the rocks, hands behind my head, looking up into the sky. I was looking for familiar constellations. Strange, my favorites were always a part of the winter sky.

Orion's glowing belt and sword, the hunter. And not too far off was his eternal prey, Taurus, the bull. I often wondered who was really the hunter in that particular battle: man seeking food and glory, or the beast seeking to destroy the alien spoiler of the land? I found myself sympathizing with the beast. That part of the country creates that kind of feeling, a feeling of helplessness and trespass. Perhaps we, as a species, have no right to come in and spoil the land. We turn the wonders of nature into amusements for our children, and what we don't try to make a buck off, we mow down, pave over and park on.

I remembered the only real feeling of oneness with the forest I had ever felt here. I had spent at least six hours climbing back into the forest, away from every commercial campsite I could see. All I knew, when I finally stopped, was that the highway was somewhere south of me. I made my camp, without a fire or anything that would betray my presence, and sat down to contemplate a tree. My urge to see the tree soon had me climbing among its branches. It was midsummer, but there was still snow on the ground, and I was sure that the bears were still groggy from their long nap. So I was very surprised and pleased to see a mother bear and her two cubs romping around in a clearing. She looked fat and lazy, content to look for insects under the log she had just turned over.

The cubs, however, were extremely excited at the prospect of playing in so new a world. They rolled and wrestled each other all over the clearing. I sat silently in my tree, knowing I was seeing something no other tourist in Wyoming could see from their neon-lit, plastic campsites.

One cub soon decided that mother really should join in their games, and went over to persuade her. She, being more concerned with practical matters, like food, ignored her impetuous offspring. The cub was not about to be ignored, and he jumped on his mother's hind end, his young bear teeth chomping right in. Mother bear, a stern disciplinarian, reared back and let go a swat with the back of her paw that knocked her uppity young'un a good twenty feet. The cub sat up in a daze. I knew that a wallop like that could easily kill a man. But it didn't seem to hurt the cub, who just shook his head and ran back to his mother and bit her again. My face must have been glowing with the smile I had at that point. I watched the mother bear, now really perturbed at her offspring, herd them together and take them from the clearing, back to whatever shelter they called home.

I smiled at the memory, a warm smile from the inside combating the night's chill. I heard footsteps behind me. Startled, I turned to see Chris standing there, her eyes almost glowing in the night, and her hands buried deep in the pocket of her warm, woolen coat. "Mind if I join you, Ken?" she asked in a hesitant tone.

"Of course not," I smiled. "Please, pull up a rock."

"You missed dinner, you know," she said. "What are you thinking about?"

"Nothing, everything, just kind of letting my mind wander," I said as she sat down next to me, the closeness of her body warming me.

"It's beautiful here," she said. "It's like God created this whole place special for people to come when they're tired of towns."

"Yeah," I said, "then people bought it from other people, sold it to other people, and the people that were left rented it and brought the towns with them."

"You're bitter, Ken," she smiled. "I guess you're right though."

"I'm sorry, Chris. I didn't mean to sound that way. I was just thinking of how it was when the first trappers came here, like John Colter, who was with the Lewis and Clark expedition. When it came time to go back, he refused and stayed out West. He was the first white man to see this place. No one believed him though. They thought he was crazy. It was known as Colter's Hell for a long time. Then Jim Bridger saw it and people began to take notice."

"Maybe I'm bitter, and I guess I shouldn't be, but I want to feel what those dudes felt, you know? A sense of discovery, of fear at being among such beautiful and magnificent works of nature. Instead, it's all cluttered up by film negatives from Polaroids. And I'm not surprised at the sights because I saw them all on the late show when I was ten."

"Hey, I'm sorry if I'm boring you," I said.

"You're not," she answered, drawing closer. "Warm me up, please, I'm cold." I put my arm over her shoulder.

"Chris," I said softly, trembling slightly as I spoke, "How come you people have let me hang around as long as I have? You planned all summer for this, and I know perfectly well that those plans didn't include me. Don't get me wrong or anything, I've been happier these last few days than I've been in a long time. I just feel like I'm horning in on your vacation, that's all."

"Do you want to leave, Ken?" she asked in a casual whisper.

"No, I don't; of course I don't. But like, you're here with me, and I take it for granted that Jay and Madilyn know where you are. Aren't they jealous--Jay at least? He might figure that I'm coming between you and him. After I'm gone, you'll still have each other. I wouldn't want to destroy that."

"No, Ken," she said with a small laugh. "Jay's one of my closest friends, and I love him dearly, but there's no possessiveness on either side. He's not jealous of you at all. In fact, when I asked about you at dinner, he was the one who told me the direction you'd gone. Madilyn feels as close to you as I do. All of us are very glad we found you. We don't want you to leave until you're ready. And you'll know when that is before we do."

"I just wish there was someway I could thank all of you for coming along when you did," I said. "After the crap that went on in Iowa, I was feeling pretty down. You folks pulled me up, saved my head. I don't know where I'd be inside my head, if you weren't with me."

"What happened, Ken? Can you talk about it?" she said in a gentle voice filled with concern.

I drew her closer and told her the long story of my search for a friend in Iowa and of a girl with sad blue eyes.

"Maybe it bothered me more than it should have," I said finally. "Maybe other people wouldn't have been hurt so much by it all."

"No, Ken," said Chris quietly. "I guess that would have hurt just about anyone. You love that girl, don't you?"

"I don't know, Chris, really I don't. Even if I did, I can't go back there."

"Why not, Ken?"

"Because I'm no good at basketball."

She sat up and looked me in the eye. "Now what's that got to do with anything?"

"Something to do with rebounds..." I said.

"Now, Ken, that's just stupid!" she answered loudly. "If you're in love, no matter how you got there, you can work things out somehow!"

I looked at Chris, wondering how to answer that kind of optimism, and sighed. "I'm just a street freak, Chris. That's not what she needs now. She's got to have somebody a hell of a lot more stable than me. Maybe the steady, straight kind of guy she can trust completely, depend on completely. That just isn't me. If I wanted that kind of life, I'd have it, but I don't. I can't ask her to share this..." I raised my hands to somehow embrace the life I was talking about. "It's not what she wants."

"So you're not going back there?" she asked.

"I can't, Chris," I said. "I just know it's better this way, and I'm sure she'll find the person she needs. And I know that ain't me."

"I think you're wrong," she said. "But I won't try to change your mind. I guess I understand how you feel. I understand as much as I can, anyway."

"Thanks, Chris," I said and leaned over and kissed her on the cheek. She turned her head, and with her soft hands, drew my lips to hers and kissed me.

Feeling like a shy school boy, I gently stroked her long hair, afraid of what to say. I reached over and picked up a small, flat stone.

"Listen," I whispered, "on the water, three skips." I skimmed the stone across the lake. It skipped twice. "Oh, well..." I grinned. She snuggled closer in the night air.

GOOD-BYE CHRISTY

The four of us continued our way west for the next couple of days, watching the mountains, green-covered with grass and trees, ending in bareness above the timber line. Above the line, streaks of snow were shining in the sun.

My affection for Chris, Madilyn and Jay grew stronger everyday under the silent monuments of the West. Our time was spent traveling along the highway, deeper into the heart of the country than the three of them had ever been before. Our voices would often blend in laughing, in glorious attempts at harmony to the accompaniment of Chris's light guitar tones. A hundred times, we embraced in spontaneous joy of being together, moving along a friendly road to nowhere in particular. The nights were spent in wonder and awe of the western sky, rolled up in my bedroll with either Chris, Madilyn or Jay, or all sharing my view of the sky.

Conversations about yesterday, tomorrow, the world, each other, stretched with happy smiles, seemed to last forever and at the same time, ended too soon.

One afternoon, while stopping for gas at a small town, Madilyn decided to call home and tell everyone that the New Jersey travelers were safe. I located a supermarket and ''liberated'' a few foodstuffs for dinner. When I returned with my spoils, I found everyone in the van broken up with laughter.

''Hey, hey, gang, what' the joke?'' I asked, breaking into a curious smile.

''Ken,'' said Jay, still laughing. ''When we left, we promised our folks we wouldn't pick up any hitchhikers.''

''Yeah?'' I asked in happy puzzelment.

''Well, the first thing Mad said when her Mom answered the phone was, 'Hi, I just called to let you know that the four of us are just fine.' '' And Jay burst into a fresh fit of laughter, joined by all of us.

''Welcome to our families!'' Chris smiled. ''They all know all about you now!''

''And from my description, they decided they liked you

too,'' broke in Madilyn.

"How about we celebrate Ken's acceptance tonight?'' asked Jay. "We'll find a place to camp, do a few numbers and drink some wine. How's that sound, folks?''

His suggestion was greeted with a cheer and a round of applause, and we spent the rest of the day looking for a suitable campsite.

By evening, we pulled the van alongside the road, a hundred miles from the nearest town. There was a range of high peaks to the west of us, breaking the horizon into a thousand different sunsets. Just off the road was a hill, and on top of the hill was a small, flat plateau, perfect for our small party.

While Chris and I fixed dinner, Jay and Madilyn ran through a large pasture, following a herd of cows. With the smoke from the fire blowing softly into her face, Chris stirred a plate of beans and chopped meat. Lifting her hair away from her face with one hand, she leaned back and said, "You know, I guess I've really missed a lot by never coming here before. I'm going to miss views like this when I go back to school.''

"It's beautiful land,'' I answered. "Sometimes I feel that I've lost touch with it. I often forget how big it really is, and...'' my voice trailed off, "...and how really beautiful.'' I hesitated, gathering wind and looking at her soft outline near the fire. "I've noticed the beauty more with you, Jay and Madilyn than I have for a long, long time.''

"I don't think you've forgotten, Ken. You've just become a part of it. Like that flower you lost in South Dakota, remember?'' she stirred the food and smiled at the fond memory. "When I think of traveling, of stops like this one, I'll think of you, because they're part of the same world.''

I looked at her, her eyes shining and a bit reddened from the smoke of the small stove. "Thanks, Chris, but you're wrong. I'm not a part of the land. I'm not a part of all that,'' I said, pointing to the pasture where Jay and Madilyn were mere dark specks against the green and brown field.

"I'm more a part of that,'' and I pointed toward the highway. "Part of the pavement, concrete sidewalks, asphalt streets, all the hard, artificial blankets we've covered the land with. I love this land, maybe because I'm from the Midwest, but I really do love it. But I'm completely separate from it. The people who were a part of it, a real part, the Indians and trappers, were all run over by the bulldozers and cement trucks. The rest of us are just lost in a blind maze of technology. We can admire the land, even love its beauty, but we'll never again be a part of it.''

Chris stood for a moment, the plate of beans in her hands, head cocked to one side, a smile on her face that reflected thoughtfulness. ''Maybe you're right,'' she said slowly. ''But I like to think of you as a part of the land, the hills, forests and meadows. Please don't try to disillusion me,'' she added with a quick, bright smile and a wink as she shut off the stove.

''My goodness,'' I laughed, ''aren't we both getting poetic tonight. I'll call the others for dinner.''

That night, with the glory of an Oregon sky stretching above us, we climbed to the plateau. Laughing, listening to Chris's guitar, occasionally breaking into a song, we smoked the last of my dope, drank a couple of bottles of cheap wine and enjoyed the evening together. Words of everlasting friendship were spoken between people who had been strangers only a week before.

We crawled into our bedrolls beneath a small mound, still able to see the sky, but sheltered from the night breezes. Chris and Jay curled up just beyond me, and Madilyn lay next to me. For awhile, we looked up at stars, talked of travel beyond the bounds of earth.

''You know, Mad, people like you are really rare. I'm going to miss you. I've been happy traveling with you. Happier than with anyone else that's picked me up,'' I said to her, still looking into the night sky.

''I do know what you mean, Ken,'' she answered quietly. ''It's been a happy time for all of us. I'm not looking forward to saying goodbye, that's for sure!'' she said in a strong whisper, turning her face to me. ''When do you plan to leave?''

''Don't know, Mad,'' I said, ''I really don't. Sometime in the next couple of days. I'll know when. Something will just tell me, and I'll know.''

''I'll be living in Boston next term,'' she said. ''If I give you my address, will you come and visit?''

''I can't promise when or anything like that, Mad,'' I said, feeling an urge to promise anything to hang on to this night forever. "But I can promise that if I'm within a thousand miles of you, I'll come to see you."

"You'd better," she said and leaned over to kiss me, her soft, warm lips on mine and our arms entwined amid the folds of the bedroll. And with the lights of countless stars above us, we closed the day.

We woke the next morning groggy and thirsty because of our night's partying. "Oh, for something to drink, my kingdom for a tall glass of orange juice!" said Jay, raising his arms above him, appealing to the god of magical orange blossoms.

"Let's go back to the van and get something for breakfast. I'm starved," said Madilyn.

"More like lunch," I said, pointing to the sky and the high sun.

Like a troop of weary soldiers, we climbed back down the hill to the highway. I carried both my pack and bedroll because I used the pack as a pillow. The rest just carried clumsy sleeping bags. When we got to the road, our mouths all fell agape at once.

We couldn't believe it, but it was true. The van was no longer there.

"Gone!" exclaimed Jay. "Where the hell could it have gone?! There's no town anywhere near here. The thing's locked up and I've got the keys! Where could it have gone?"

We checked and found that the van hadn't rolled down the hill to the pasture. It had definitely been stolen. Feeling afraid for my friends, I sat down on a nearby rock. I couldn't think of what to do. We couldn't hitch together. Four of us would never get a ride. There was no phone around to call for help. In short, we were stranded. And I couldn't help at all. It was one thing to be stuck someplace alone. That had happened often enough, but yet another thing to be stuck with three other people who needed help.

I unlashed my pack and got out my canteen, which was still nearly filled. "Come here and have a drink," I called. After finishing the water, we talked. "Where's the nearest town east of here?" I asked.

"The one where we bought the wine," said Chris, "about seventy five miles back. Why?"

"Well," I said, "the nearest one west is about a hundred. We've got to hitch to one of them and look up the local constable.''

"How? Nobody's going to pick up four of us, especially looking as dirty as we look now after sleeping up there last night," said Chris.

"Shit, all of our money, everything is in that van," said Jay, almost to himself.

"O.K.," I said, "we'll try it this way: I don't need money and shit like that, so here." And I gave Jay the four dollars in my wallet. Then I tossed my pack to Madilyn. "You'll find clean sweaters and shirts enough for all of you there. It should help your appearance. You're right about the four of us not getting rides, so I'll head west to that town alone. You three go east to the other. Two chicks and a guy should do all right. Once we get to the towns, we give all the information we can to the cops on both ends. That will give them about a hundred and seventy five miles of road to cover."

"If anybody picked the thing up and trashed it, they should find it. I'll stay in my town until I hear from you. Just call the police station there and let me know you're all right and have reported the thing missing. Then I'll split. Once you've contacted me on your own, the cops will help you out all they can. If you find the van, look for me on the road. If not, it's up to you, O.K.?" I said in an excited voice, hoping that by some incredible piece of luck they would find their property intact.

Chris looked at me, then said deliberately, "Why give us everything you have? Why don't you come with us?"

"Look, you know why," I said. "You three have to stay together to decide what you're going to do. I'd just be a drag on you. You helped me when I needed you, so now let me be of some kind of help in return."

Without waiting for a reply, I turned to Jay to get all the information on the van that would help the police find it.

I got my bedroll in order and threw it on my back. I turned to the three of them standing behind me. They all looked afraid and worried. "Hey, look," I said. "It's only property, even if you never get it back, so what? You're still some pretty beautiful people, and nothing's going to change that." I glanced at my pack lying at Madilyn's feet; the pack, to me, was as important as the van was to them, and as they had shared their property, I could share mine.

Skipping anymore goodbyes, I ran across the highway

and began walking west.

It wasn't a large town, the downtown area wasn't filled with shining plate glass department stores. Instead the stores were small, made of aging, dark brick and wood. I looked for an official building. Court houses and police stations were usually the most solid, stately looking buildings around. Besides the columns and large grey stones, these buildings were generally marked by a large flag hanging from a pole in front.

I found the station within a few minutes and walked in. Tossing my bedroll into a corner, I walked over to the desk where a wiry man in a dark uniform sat. He looked at me, his eyes narrowing slightly, and put down the pencil he'd been writing with.

"How do, chief," I said in a cheery voice. The irony of being in a police station of my own free will was almost comical if it hadn't been for my friends' loss.

With that van, Jay, Chris and Madilyn had hoped to experience, at least for a time, the freedom that the confines of jobs and school did not allow. Now, with it stolen, the freedom they'd purchased with a summer's worth of work was gone. It seemed strange to me that freedom could be purchased with property. But that's how they saw it, and I couldn't change their minds, even if I'd wanted to.

The policeman behind the desk nodded in response to my greeting and asked, "What can I do for you, son?" His voice sounded weary, and it seemed that all police desk jockies were constantly bored and overworked at the same time. They never seemed happy to fill out the forms for which I was responsible.

"I'd like to report a theft, sir," I said.

An hour later, I was slowly shuffling my way along a side street toward a small park. Something I had always loved about the West was that constant presence of the mountains. No matter how drab the town, how dull the company, the skyline always loomed high and beautiful.

It wasn't a large park. Like the town, it was small and plain. I lay my bedroll on the grass and sat down in a swing. It was a nice, simple swing, belonging to the park. Rather than made out of chain and rubber, it was hung by rope, and the seat was wooden. I leaned my head back and slowly started pumping, creating a breeze to break the growing heat of the day.

I thought of the past week, the slow-rolling along the highway and the warm friendship of travel. I had forgotten to get their addresses. I guess it didn't matter. I knew I would never see them again. The past week would forever be nothing but another pleasant memory.

Maybe that was what was wrong with Trans-Amerika. A life of nothing but a series of encounters. Some good, some bad, all short. I knew it was easy to live that way, easy and empty.

My mind raced back to a hundred faces, laughing faces, faces with tear-stained cheeks, and faces full of hate and fear; the faces of Trans-Amerika.

As I remembered, I allowed my mind to linger on one face. Blond hair curving softly around a pale, smiling face. Blue eyes shining and laughing, a gentle mouth with a rare smile able to erase the darkness of my loneliness. When we were together, sharing a load of sorrow too big for one person alone, she seldom smiled. Now, over a thousand miles away, all I remembered, or wanted to remember, was the brightness that a smile could bring to her face.

I shook my head, trying to discipline my mind. I knew I would never see Mel again, anymore than I would see Chris, Madilyn or Jay again. But lingering on memories of what might have been or could have been wouldn't do me any good at all, at the present. Even as I tried to concentrate my thoughts, my mind fixed on one town and what she might be doing there at the moment.

With a slight laugh, I left the swing and wandered to the other side of the park. I reached into my pocket for a little dope and found it empty. With nothing much to do while I waited for my phone call, I curled up under a tree and fell asleep.

I rolled over a long time later, my heavy eyelids slowling opening. The sun was beginning to set, making the sky a deeper color. I looked to the distant skyline, feeling small and helpless beneath the peaks. A panoramic display of hues splashing on colors filled the early evening sky. Behind, above and around each separate point and mound of the mountains was a light show filling its section of the sky. I smiled in wonder and slowly got to my feet, reaching for my gear.

Shouldering my pack, I started walking toward the police station. I shook my head, thinking of finding a new pack, scrounging for clothes and money. California, more of Oregon, what did I want to see next? Where did I want to go next? Who would I meet next?

I looked down the street to the police station. I didn't like cop shops; they made me nervous. I would be glad to be out of their station and out of the town. As I looked down the street, I stopped; my arms fell to my sides like puppet arms when the strings snap. My mouth must have fallen open and my eyes bugged out. There, out in front of the police station, were Chris, Madilyn and Jay, laughing and waving at me.

Breaking into a run, I threw my bedroll aside and in a second, Chris's arms were around me as Jay and Madilyn slapped me on the back. Blubbering in surprise, it took a moment for the words to come out coherently. ''What are you dudes doing here?'' I managed to stammer.

''O.K., let's go sit down someplace and we'll tell you,'' said Jay with a broad grin.

We trooped over to a small restaurant and took our places around the booth. Jay ordered coffee, and with a wink, said to me, ''The coffee's on you--remember?''

I nodded, smiled and asked, ''All right, all ready, group, tell me about it. Why are you here? What about your bus?''

''Well,'' said Jay, ''we went to the other town to report it, like you said. It seems that you made better time than we did, and the cops there had already heard.''

''I guess I'm lucky,'' I said as the waitress delivered the coffee.

Jay grinned at me and continued, ''Anyway, the local Elks Club here heard about what happened.''

''WHAT?!'' I broke in, surprised.

''Yeah,'' said Madilyn, ''the cops told them.''

''Right,'' said Jay, ''and they offered to put us up here until we hear about the van. So here we are. We knew you'd be waiting for our call, so we decided to wait for you.''

''You're not gutting out on us that easily, Ken. We won't let you,'' laughed Chris.

I looked down at my coffee, then again at my three friends. I hadn't noticed it before, but both Chris and Jay were wearing shirts from my pack, a little large for Chris, but really a fair fit. Madilyn was wearing a dark sweater of mine, and I felt a warm glow of happiness creep over me. I was glad to be sharing what I had with these people.

The Elks Club had given Jay permission to buy a meal, on them, at any restaurant in town, so we ordered. I felt strange, accepting a gift from the Elks and couldn't help wondering if their generosity would be the same if they knew me, or if all of us were black. I didn't press the matter, though. I just dug into the free meal. They were worried, afraid of being stuck three thousand miles from home without money or transportation. The talk consisted of how to get home if the van wasn't found, who to call for money and who would worry the most at home. I couldn't add anything to what they were saying, so I kept silent, enjoying the meal their misfortune had brought my way.

Half way through the meal, the waitress approached Jay, telling him he had a phone call. Curious, we all watched him go behind the counter. In a minute, he came racing back to the table, jumping up, clicking his heels and throwing his head back in laughter.

"Wheeee!" he laughed. "We're going to get the mother back!"

"How?" I said in an excited voice.

"It seems that for the last week there's been an old T-Bird sitting in the very same spot we parked the van," he laughed. "Well, last night, the cops decided to haul it in."

"But somebody already moved it, and the klutz they sent out to tow it away didn't know the difference. He hauled the van away! My god, what a sap; a Ford van is not a Thunderbird!" And Jay let out another joyous laugh that we all joined.

Two days later, early in the evening, we made camp in the Redwood National Forest of California. The first look at the ocean earlier in the day had an almost numbing effect on me. From the ripe corn fields of Iowa, to the muddy slopes of South Dakota, to the shores of the great Pacific. It had been the longest ride I had ever accepted and one of the happiest. Now we seemed to have run out of land, and the feeling I had known would come to me, did. It came in the form of an ocean, an end of a paved, white-lined highway. It was time for me to leave.

The campsites in the Redwood Forest are expensive, but unlike the trailers and monstrosities of Yellowstone, the sites were set up with human beings in mind.

Large redwood tree trunks separated each campsite, a layer of damp moss covered everything and the silence and peace was so deep that anyone walking through quickly became a part of it.

I smiled through my inward feelings of fear as I gathered wood for a fire. It was quiet here, a kind of end-of-journey peace, and the gentle unbroken silence of the place made me smile with gratitude. Yet, beneath the peace and silence, was a raging, screaming fear inside me. I didn't want to be alone again. I didn't want to say goodbye again. The thought of walking alone down a city street toward nothing frightened me more now than it ever had before.

I leaned over to pick up a piece of wood I dropped accidently while my mind was wandering, and I heard a soft rustle. Looking up, I found myself eye-to-eye with a young fawn.

Taken by surprise, I drew back. And in response, the small animal came forward one tiny step. It looked so soft and delicate with its huge, brown ears twitching at the slightest sound. It's eyes were large, soft and brown and blinked at me when I nodded my head. The fawn had lost its protective spots, but a coat of light buff brown proved that a mature deer would soon replace the awkward fawn in front of me. I reached over to a nearby tree and pulled off a couple of leaves. Slowly, carefully, I leaned toward the deer, offering food in exchange for trust.

"Hi, there, little fella, how are you?" I said softly, coaxing it closer. "Where's your mother? You're kind of young and gangly to be poking around alone, aren't you?"

As I talked, the fawn hesitantly nibbled at the leaves. I could feel its warm breath on my hand, which was trembling slightly. I looked over to the van and saw Chris walking along side it.

"Psst! Chris," I whispered. "Come here." Her face broke into a wide silent smile. She tenderly walked toward us. Reaching into the pocket of her jacket, she pulled out a small paper packet of sugar from a restaurant we stopped at that morning. She emptied the sugar into her palm and held it out to the baby deer.

"Hello, little fawn, I'm not going to hurt you. No...I wouldn't hurt anything as precious as you," she cooed gently. "Kenny," she said in an excited whisper as the fawn licked her palm. "I think he likes me!"

"You or the sugar, maybe both," I grinned.

After finishing the sugar, the fawn backed up a couple of steps, and with a twitch of its small tail, it was gone back into the forest.

"Oh, Kenny," said Chris, still whispering, "it was so beautiful, so fragile."

After dinner that night, we sat by the fire for awhile. We exchanged stories and smiles; Chris played her guitar until her hands got cold. "The nights by the ocean really get chilly, don't they?" she said, holding her hands over the fire.

"Yeah," I answered, "but it's really not a biting cold, and in the morning, it warms up pretty fast."

"Well, it's a little cold for me," said Madilyn. "I'm going to sleep in the van tonight. Do you want to squeeze in too, Ken?"

"No," I smiled. "I really like California nights. It's been awhile since I've been here, and I think I'll stay out and enjoy it."

"Go ahead, man," said Jay with a friendly smile, "but as for me, it's been a long day, and I think I'll crash out now. Good night. I'll see you in the morning. Providing you're not frozen." He patted me quickly on my shoulder and I nodded in response.

An hour later, both Madilyn and Jay were fast asleep in the van, leaving Chris and me by the fire. She was silently staring into the flames, her hands deep in the pockets of her coat. I unrolled my bedroll, took out my blanket and draped it around her shoulders. She squeezed my hand as I touched her shoulders, and continued staring into the fire.

I got up and gathered two large pieces of wood to stoke the fire. "Here, sit on this," I said, putting my unrolled bedroll in front of the fire. "It's warmer." Without a word, she took her place beside me on the mat. We sat there in silence for a time, watching the flames lick the wood, glowing in bright yellow and red, throwing shadows at our feet and playing color games in our eyes.

Chris drew the blanket around her and lowered her head into my lap. Rolling over and looking into my eyes, she smiled, a soft petal-like smile. The light of the fire made her face and hair shine in the dark; her eyes were shining from the inside outward. She absently began braiding the fringe on the breast of my leather jacket. Looking past me into the sky, she said, "I can't see the stars tonight, Ken."

"I know," I said, "the trees are too high."

I looked into the fire again. The wood was all in flames now, red, yellow, orange and blue with dark red coals beneath them. It had seemed so long ago when I met my friends. A summer vacation had taken Chris to Iowa, and from Iowa a summer friendship, and then to love. As I gently stroked Chris's long hair and stared into the California campfire, the cornfields, the pain of Iowa seemed so very far away.

I couldn't imagine Chris in any other place. Not hurrying from class to class in school, or living in a New Jersey home. All I wanted to remember, the only way I could think of her, was with a campfire reflected in her face and warm eyes at night.

We had run out of land, and in a way, out of places to go together. From California, her road would take her back to New Jersey, away from the shores and from me. I couldn't go back with her and the others; I couldn't recapture the joys of first discovery. A second-time attempt at it would just be trying to catch a series of moments that would only happen once.

The end of the trip wouldn't be a soft, warm campfire in the middle of a forest. It would be a house, a city, pavement, cars, trucks, bus schedules and people close to her in a way I could never be. People who never saw her by a campfire, or feeding deer, or befriending a street freak in the middle of Amerika. In turn, the woman they knew, they were close to, was a woman I would never know either. Our time together was to be brief, a short time when two worlds could merge and share a flame in the night.

I looked into the fire, smaller flames now as the wood turned slowly to glowing embers. Despite the reasons I had to leave, I didn't want to. I had found a peace, a gentle warming of my soul with these people, and that was something I would have liked to hang onto forever, even though I knew I never could.

She drew closer to me as the warmth of the fire diminshed. I leaned over and gently kissed her. She turned up to me and returned my kiss. Then she put her arms around my waist and buried her head in the leather folds of my jacket. Holding her tightly, my hand continued to stroke her hair, warm from the fire and soft to my touch.

The flames were almost gone from the fire, the wood turning to glowing, shining coals. I hadn't told anyone that I planned to leave and now, in the cold and dark of the night, with her body pressed so closely to mine, I didn't want to tell Chris. I knew I had to, though. I had to tell her and force myself to face the reality of a lonely tomorrow.

I gently drew her face toward me, a soft face, wet with tears, and I kissed her again and wiped away the tears. I was confused. I didn't understand why she was crying, but I knew I couldn't. I knew that now, this moment, would have to be our forever memory of each other.

"Chris," I said in a soft whisper, "I've got to be leaving tomorrow."

She shook her head slightly and retreated again into the folds of my jacket. "I know," she said in a choked voice. "I've known all day."

Her arms tight around my waist and with both of my hands holding her head, I looked into the fire, a pile of dark red glowing embers now, the flames all gone, the wood consumed.

SAN FRANCISCO DARKNESS

I looked at the buildings of the Oakland street, large, made of wood and brick, both faded with age and weather. My mind slowly made its way along the past couple of days. The people from New Jersey were gone, traveling south in their van. I smiled at the memory, a warmth inside me grew until it filled every part of my being. I had never stayed with any ride as long as I had with those people. The usual feeling of emptiness after saying good-bye was even more intense now after a week's happiness. As well as emptiness I felt something else, a thankfulness for a seven day collage of wonderful memories. I wondered where they were now, if they were happy, still sharing songs along the highway.

"As usual," I thought, shaking the memories from my head, "that was then and this is now." A pair of well dressed young men came walking toward me. Their hair was fashionably shaggy, barely covering their ears and collars, their well-pressed suits were double breasted with wide lapels, just like the fashion magazines showed. Approaching them with my best street freak manner, a combination of contempt and sincerity, I said, "Hey man, like I just hit town and I'm broke. Could you spare a little change?"

"Where you from, kid?" asked one, as he curiously eyed my packs.

"Midwest, man, Iowa, Minnesota, ya know."

"Yeah, I know," he answered flipping me a quarter; his partner not to be outdone handed me a smooth crisp dollar bill.

"Well, thank you, dudes, and have a nice day," I said in surprise. Bills are an extreme rarity in the panhandling world. Actually, I wasn't in desperate need of money. The first morning I had come to Oakland after leaving my New Jersey friends, I had stumbled across a small group of employees of the city repair crew. They were laying a sidewalk; they looked undermanned and I quickly volunteered my services. They chose to ignore my lack of union credentials and experience and let me lend a hand. A

few hours later we were finished, and they gave me five
dollars.

I felt fine this morning, my walk had a light skip to it, the
packs didn't feel too heavy on my back. I had money; I was in
California, Oakland; the memories of Iowa would be
submerged here on the pavement of the city. I laughed as I
skipped along the street; this was where I belonged, this was
who I was. I was just another street freak, panhandling my
way through life. The pain of broken hopes and shattered
futures belonged to someone else; they had nothing to do
with me.

A battered pick-up filled with lumber stopped at the
intersection ahead of me. The driver, a stocky freak with
shoulder length blond hair topped by a leather sombrero,
stared at me. I looked at him and grinned, threw my packs on
the sidewalk and stood with my hands on my hips, my grin
turned to a laugh in response to his finger pointing at me. He
was called Reese, one of Oakland's finer artists, a magician
with wire, neon lights and a paint brush. He was married to
the sister of a girl I had known long ago. She and I had split,
but the friendship I had established with her brother-in-law
had stayed.

His beard parted in a smile and he called out to me.
Carrying my gear, I hurried to the truck and threw the packs
in the back with the lumber. Once inside, we quickly
exchanged the traditional handclasp. "Good Lord, Kenny,
what the hell are you doing here? I haven't seen you since,
when was it?" he muttered, scratching his head. "Sometime
around late June wasn't it, about two, two and a half months
ago!"

"Yeah, man, around that," I grinned, "I was just
heading for your place. How goes your world?"

A car behind us honked, and Reese pulled ahead into the
Oakland traffic.

"Good thing I saw you when I did," he said in a serious
voice. "I don't live there anymore; my old lady and I busted
up about a month ago. I was just over there to use the
shower. Some friends and I are renting a loft, but we ain't got
any plumbing yet."

"I'm sorry to hear that man, I really am!" I said.

"Don't worry, Ken, we'll get plumbing," he said with a
grin.

"Not plumbing," I laughed. "I'm sorry about your marriage."

"I know, Ken. Hey, dude, ya staying long?"

"Don't know. Can I flop at your loft tonight?" I asked.

"Sure thing," he said, "you got a number? I'm out."

"No, I'm sorry. I just hit town and ain't had time to cop, or the coin either."

"Well, I've got a few bucks," he said as he parked the truck by a large warehouse.

"O.K., let's pool 'em. I'll pop over to Berkely and cop a lid," I said.

"Fine, here's five," he said, handing me a bill. "I'll be upstairs; just ring the bell. How long you gonna' be gone?"

"Berkely's not far," I said. "call it an hour."

Berkely is a dope buyers' paradise. The street drugs are generally of pretty good quality, providing the buyer knows that anything in a tab or cap is probably acid, not mescaline, THC, or any of the rest of the promised organic highs.

Every third freak on the street, is dealing something or other. In Berkely there is really one street, Telegraph Avenue, full of shops selling records, posters, incense, wines, natural foods, and leather shops catering to the biker set. The sidewalks were littered with the citizens of Trans-Amerika, rapping to each other, staring aimlessly into nothing, or spare changing the passing straights. I shook my head in an affirmative response as I surveyed the scene. The needle-like pinnacle marking Sproul Plaza stood marking the campus like a giant monument to all that Berkely stood for. Thinking of Berkely's past, I glanced to the right and the fenced off lot that had once been Peoples' Park. The lot, with its basketball hoops and paved playground, was empty. In over two years since the battle for the park, no one had desecrated its memory by walking on the ground that had become almost sacred. Students would walk two blocks around it to keep the memories of shotguns, helicopters and the bloody body of James Rector intact.

Berkely was a lot of things to all the people of Trans-Amerika; to me this moment, it was a smorgasbord of illegal highs. Person after person would pass whispering, "hash, weed, acid."

Reese's loft was the top floor of one of the countless warehouses in Oakland. A large room filled with lumber and tools and the starts of several partitions marked what the loft soon would be.

He took the knife from his side and cut off two large pieces of bread from one of the several loaves sitting on a table. Handing me one of the pieces, he said, "You know, Ken, when Kathy and I were married, we had all the plans in the world."

I looked up from my seat on the floor and the joint I was rolling and shook my head in response.

"I don't know what went wrong," he continued. "The last few months we just sort of drifted apart. Maybe she wanted something I couldn't give her. If she did, she never said anything. Maybe I was supposed to know?" He looked at me, then shrugged his shoulders.

"Hey man, light that. I'll be right back," he said tossing me a book of matches.

I mumbled something and lit the number, taking a deep hit, forcing the smoke deep into my lungs. I thought, "It's the same all over." I shook my head, exhaled the smoke. No matter where I was, the same things existed; the pain of trashed expectations was universal. The hurt in a woman's eyes two thousand miles away visited me here through Reese's eyes.

He returned with a bottle of warm white wine and after taking a deep pull handed it to me. "Mmm, thanks. What are your plans, fella." I said, handing him the shining joint.

"Keep working on my art. That's all I really want to do anyway. Like, I'm an artist, Ken. That's not any sort of brag; it's just the truth. I guess all the love and emotion I should have put into my marriage, I put into my work. Now that the marriage is gone, all I've got left is the art, so I'll concentrate on that."

"You've got something then, Reese," I said. "What about your old lady?"

"I'm not sure. There's some executive dude she's been seeing. They could do all right." The joint had gone out in his hand, and he paused to relight it. "I'm not jealous; really I'm not. I hope she'll be happy. If she couldn't find it with me, then I won't stop her from looking some place else."

I nodded in agreement. Reese wasn't bitter, just resigned to the acceptance of something he couldn't change. The conversation drifted into other channels, and with the help of the weed and wine, we were soon laughing our way down a trail of memories.

The next night, as I was making my way along the garbage-strewn streets of the city, I found my mind as usual wandering back to a town and a girl in Iowa. I had never found myself constantly thinking about someone before. When I slept, her eyes would shine their way through all my dreams. When I was awake, I would wonder what she was doing at that moment.

"Mel," I muttered to myself as I kicked an old whisky bottle into the gutter, "could you be happy with me? Could you love me? Are you thinking of me now?" I shook my head; I knew she couldn't love me. I had nothing to offer her; I had no future, no skills, no money. All the things that she needed to make her happy, I had no way of giving her. I tried to be like Reese, resigned to something I couldn't change. If I would just accept the fact that there was no way for her to find happiness with me, then I could forget her.

Instead of resigning myself to the hopelessness of the situation, I kept filling my thoughts with imaginary plans, imaginary jobs, imaginary hopes in the heart of Amerika.

I stepped to the side to avoid two men walking toward me. Lost in my thoughts, I didn't notice them turn around and begin to follow me.

Whap! A blinding light flashed in my head and my knees crumpled. As I began to fall I found myself being shoved against the wall, and I felt the point of steel against my throat.

"Don't move, muther, and you won't get hurt!" I heard a far-off voice say as a pair of rough hands went through my pockets, pulling out my wallet.

My head was spinning; I could hardly see or hear. If it weren't for the arms of one of my assailants holding me against the hard brick of a building, I would have been laying on the sidewalk.

"Hey Man, you hippie!" the far-off voice shouted. "All you got is two dollars?!"

"You hit him hard, man," I heard another far-off voice say. "He can't talk. Let's take what he's got and split."

"Man, he only got two fucking dollars!"

"O.K., then let's take the two and go!"

"What about the coat? It's good leather."

"Forget it! Let's get the fuck out of here. Come on man, let's go!''

The arms released me, and I quickly crumpled to the sidewalk. Just before my face hit the pavement, a boot connected with my cheek, crashing me back to the wall, and in a second I was out, asleep in my own blood.

Waking up in a few minutes, I grabbed my stomach and felt my body vomiting up anything inside it and continuing in dry heaves when the stomach was empty.

When the spasms had finished, I staggered along until I reached Reese's door and fell on the doorbell.

"Ken, hey dude," I heard a voice say, a voice much closer, and when I opened my eyes, Reese's smiling face was clear in my mind, reflected from the bare bulb above us.

"Hi, Reese," I managed, "a couple of your local citizens just popped me pretty good."

His face broke into a large smile, then into a laugh.

"Ken, you lucky bastard," he laughed. "Man, count yourself lucky just being alive. The cats around here generally don't leave anybody walking, especially whitey."

I slowly sat up feeling my stomach quivering again. I put my hand on my throbbing head, feeling a large welt in the back. "Well," I mumbled, "I guess I lead a charmed life." I looked at Reese's smiling face and laughed out loud, forgetting the pain.

"Yeah, you do, man," he said, "you really do. Here, lucky fella, you were carrying this when I came downstairs," he said and tossed me my wallet. "Money aside, everything seems to be intact."

I stood up on shaky legs and began to walk around the room, letting the dizziness leave my head. The weak feeling in my stomach was soon gone too. "Reese," I muttered, "Before I got nailed, I was thinking about something, someone actually." I sat down cross-legged on a small table and reached into my shirt pocket for some dope and papers. "They didn't even take my weed," I chuckled, with a shake of my aching head.

"Anyway, like I was saying," I continued, "I was thinking of a chick in Iowa that I got to know while I was there a couple of weeks ago." I stopped talking for a moment and concentrated on the number I was rolling, uncertain about how to continue. "Like, do you ever think about your old lady? I mean, not just thinking of her casually, but like when you're doing something, do you wonder what she's doing at that very moment?"

"Of course I do," he answered offering me a lighted match for the joint. "I guess that's kind of universal for anybody strung out on anyone else. This girl must really be something for you to start getting that way about her, especially when you're a couple of thousand miles away."

"Yeah," I answered with a small grin as I exhaled a lung full of smoke. "She's quite a woman. I'm not sure why, but I've had her bouncing around in my brain for a whole lot of miles."

"So, why'd you leave her?" he asked.

"I guess I was just afraid of being cut down. Like you may not have been everything your wife wanted in an old man, but at least you can look at her and the world and say, 'I am an artist; this is who I am.' But I can't even offer her that. Like I kind of wandered into her life and wandered out, well skipped out, actually," I quickly added.

"Well, man," said Reese, "I can't tell you what to do, of course, but it sure seems like if you would have tried to get it on with her and didn't make it, you wouldn't be any worse off than you are now."

"Maybe you're right," I answered. "Maybe I didn't want to risk spoiling something we had. It was kind of neat," I muttered as I unlaced my leather wrist band and laid it on the table next to me and leaned up against the wall and took a long hit on the weed. I closed my eyes,letting the dope rush through my head,exchanging the pain of the blow for the fluffy fogginess of marijuana smoke.

"It was neat," I said with my eyes closed. "She needed me. Like she didn't just want me around because I was a nice guy and good entertainment--she really did need me."

"Hey, dude, who got his skull cracked tonight," said Reese with a small understanding smile. "Let's get some sleep."

"Thanks man. Really Reese, thanks a lot for everything. You know, saving my ass out there, listening to my rambling and well, you know, just everything."

"Yeah, I know," he said smiling. "You gonna' hang around for a while?"

"No man, thanks, but I think I'll kind of drift north and

look at a few beaches.''

The sun was just rising behind me as I stared into the waves. Slowly and with a steady rhythm they made their way to the land. It had been a cold night wrapped in my bed roll, but the day promised to be warm. I unbuttoned my shirt, stood up and turned around to meet the morning. Stretching my arms and embracing the sun, I smiled and sat down again.

I was at the end of the land. The highways of Trans-Amerika all ended here. Their white lines and signs were washed by the forever expanse of moving water. I idly drew my name in the sand with the point of my knife--Kenny--and below the name, as usual, I wrote Trans-Amerika.

As I sat there my mind wandered back to the place it had often returned during the last few weeks. Iowa, corn stalks, a blond-haired girl, the heart of Amerika. I didn't know how to avoid Amerika anymore. I remembered riding through Nevada two years earlier, looking at the mounds of colored sand rising sharp against a bright blue sky. I had become lost in the view and my verbal response to my aesthetic thrill was ''scenery like that almost makes you forget there's a war on.''

The war was still on, and I was still drifting through a land of beauty hoping to forget the ugliness in the world. The pain of trash-loves, the horror of stock-supported napalm, the thud of a policeman's club on my back, the tears of a million people asking why. I looked slowly around me to a large log laying dead on the beach about fifteen feet from where I sat. I looked at the log, then quickly flipped my knife, handle to blade in my hand. Then with a swift flash of my arm, I flung the weapon and nodded at the quivering handle, the blade imbedded over an inch in the wood.

I was alone on a beach flinging my knife against an enemy I had been trying to avoid for a long time. There was a world of love, of pain, of reality I hadn't been a part of for a long time. The time and distance I had covered hadn't changed that world in the least. I retrieved my knife, sheathed it, flung my packs over my shoulder and headed toward the highway.

I remembered an old hobo philosophy I had heard once, ''Go west'' they said, ''but all they meant was go home.''

The fog of the Bay City was just beginning to slowly creep over the city as I made my way along a narrow street. Stopping into a small drug store, I bought a stamp to go along with the envelope, pen and paper I'd ripped off in another store.

Stepping out of the doorway into the chill of the night, I made my way through the streets again. Looking to the top of the hill, I saw a lone street light on the corner. The fog hadn't climbed that high yet, so I headed toward it. I loved San Francisco fogs, cool, damp and thick. Walking along, watching my body heat melt the mist just in front of me, I tunneled my way through the fog toward the light. Buildings loomed above me like sleeping giants of the mist. To my left was another tunnel coming toward me, a quick word, a raised hand signaled momentary friendship.

I sat down under the light, pulled my knees up to my chest. I lit a number and let the smoke take my mind slowly along the path I had chosen to follow. A path that would take me back to the roots of myself and the land called Amerika.

My eyes wandered to the glowing lights of Fisherman's Wharf, almost hidden in the fog below. I wished the smell of steamed crab and lobster would be blown my way by a friendly wind. The friendly thought of warmth and food brought back memories of a girl far away. I held a lungful of smoke deep inside myself as I let my mind gently fondle the memory. Her face, her smile, the feeling of her touch had followed me over two thousand miles.

I wanted to tell her that I loved her and would be coming back to Iowa soon. I wanted to see her at least once more and have her know that I wanted more than a casual Trans-Amerikan friendship. I couldn't tell her why, because I didn't know myself. Maybe I wanted to be needed by her; maybe I wanted to feel the stability of Iowa responsibilities.

I wanted her to know that I was offering what I had never offered before; a love that I would try to work at and build and rebuild day after day. I had tried to run away from her, but found her memory couldn't be erased by drugs or distance. I wanted her to know I wasn't running anymore. I was coming back to Iowa and to her.

I wondered what she would think when she got the letter. I had never written to anyone before, while I was on the road. Trans-Amerika leaves no forwarding addresses for its freaks.

Lonely again, I needed her presence to end that feeling. She needed me, or at least once she did. I didn't know, and I wasn't even sure about that. Something unexplainable, something powerful, made me love her.

"Strange," I thought, "I don't really remember telling a girl that I loved her. I guess I have, but anyone in the past doesn't seem to matter."

I put my pen to the paper. The fog crept over the paper and my hand, dampening the sheet and making the ink skip. My hand was trembling as I began. A sentence on a sheet of paper, written in a fog on a San Francisco street, was going to totally change my life.

It wasn't just a letter, and it wasn't just the admittance of love. It was something that as a Trans-Amerikan freak, I had never done before. It was the making of a commitment. A determination to go back to something, to be willing to take hold of someone and feel love together. Not just a one-moment, one-day love, but the forever and ever kind of love that Mel wanted and expected.

With a smile known only to myself, I looked at the sheet of paper and its ink-blotted scribblings. I nodded silently as I reached for the envelope and stamp. I grinned as I noticed that the number had gone out in my hand.

I addressed the letter, struggled with the damp stamp and slipped it in the pocket of my jacket. I threw my packs on my back and began walking toward an eastbound highway. I stopped at a mailbox, threw the letter in, and continued on my way.